THE NEW MERMAIDS

A Fair Quarrel

DISCARD

THE NEW MERMAIDS

General Editors
PHILIP BROCKBANK
Professor of English, University of York

BRIAN MORRIS
Professor of English, University of Sheffield

A Fair Quarrel

THOMAS MIDDLETON
AND
WILLIAM ROWLEY

Edited by R. V. HOLDSWORTH

ERNEST BENN LIMITED
LONDON

First published in this form 1974
by Ernest Benn Limited
25 New Street Square, Fleet Street, London, EC4A 3JA
& Sovereign Way, Tonbridge, Kent
© *Ernest Benn Limited 1974*
Distributed in Canada by
The General Publishing Company Limited, Toronto
Printed in Great Britain

ISBN 0 510-34107-1

Paperback 0 510-34108-X

TO
MY PARENTS

CONTENTS

ACKNOWLEDGEMENTS

I AM PLEASED to acknowledge the help and kindness of Professor Dame Helen Gardner, who supervised my work on the play in Oxford three years ago. During the same period of research Mr J. B. Bamborough read and commented on the explanatory notes, and Mr D. F. Foxon advised in matters textual and bibliographical. I am grateful to them both for their guidance and encouragement.

I should also like to thank Miss Clare Colvin for much assistance during the final stages; Miss Margaret Pelling for information about Jacobean medicine; Miss Eva Wagner and Mrs Vera Zamagni for translating German theses and Italian source material; Mr M. P. Jackson, who put at my disposal his valuable linguistic data on the Middleton–Rowley collaboration; Mr Peter Stephens for advice about Cornish customs; Dr John Carey and Mr D. G. Neill for some helpful suggestions; the Provost and Fellows of Eton College; and, not least, Miss Marlene LeBrun and Dr J. J. G. Alexander for their saint-like patience.

Manchester
February 1974

R. V. H.

ABBREVIATIONS

1. *Texts of* A Fair Quarrel

Q1	first edition, 1617.
Q2	second edition, 1622.
Lamb	C. Lamb, ed., *Specimens of English Dramatic Poets*, 1808 (extracts).
Dyce	A. Dyce, ed., *The Works of Thomas Middleton*, 5 vols., 1840.
Bullen	A. H. Bullen, ed., *The Works of Thomas Middleton*, 8 vols., 1885–86.
Ellis	H. Ellis, ed., *Thomas Middleton*, The Mermaid Series, 2 vols., 1887–90.
Sampson	M. W. Sampson, ed., *Thomas Middleton*, New York, 1915.
Oliphant	E. H. C. Oliphant, ed., *Shakespeare and his Fellow Dramatists*, 2 vols., New York, 1929.

2. *The works of Middleton and Rowley*

Middleton: Bullen's text has been used, supplemented with the following:

The Puritan	C. F. Tucker Brooke, ed., *The Shakespeare Apocrypha*, 1908.

Rowley:

A Cure for a Cuckold	F. L. Lucas, ed., *The Complete Works of John Webster*, 4 vols., 1927.
A New Wonder, a Woman Never Vexed	W. C. Hazlitt, ed., *Dodsley's Old English Plays*, 15 vols., 1874–76.
All's Lost by Lust and *A Shoemaker, a Gentleman*	C. W. Stork, ed., *William Rowley his All's Lost by Lust and A Shoemaker, a Gentleman with an Introduction on Rowley's Place in the Drama*, Philadelphia, 1910.

3. *Other works*

Bentley	G. E. Bentley, *The Jacobean and Caroline Stage*, 7 vols., 1941–68.
Chambers	E. K. Chambers, *The Elizabethan Stage*, 4 vols., 1923.
Dekker	F. Bowers, ed., *The Dramatic Works of Thomas Dekker*, 4 vols., 1953–61.

Fletcher	A. Glover, ed., *The Works of Francis Beaumont and John Fletcher*, 10 vols., 1905–12.
H & S	C. H. Herford and P. and E. Simpson, eds., *The Works of Ben Jonson*, 11 vols., 1925–52.
Heywood	[R. H. Shepherd, ed.,] *The Dramatic Works of Thomas Heywood*, 6 vols., 1874.
Marston	H. H. Wood, ed., *The Plays of John Marston*, 3 vols., 1934–39.
Nashe	R. B. McKerrow, ed., *The Works of Thomas Nashe*, 5 vols., 1904–10.
OED	*The Oxford English Dictionary*.
Partridge	E. Partridge, *Shakespeare's Bawdy*, rev. edn., 1968.
Shakespeare	P. Alexander, ed., *The Complete Works of William Shakespeare*, 1951.
Sugden	E. H. Sugden, *A Topographical Dictionary to the Works of Shakespeare and his Fellow Dramatists*, 1925.
Tilley	M. P. Tilley, *A Dictionary of the Proverbs in England in the Sixteenth and Seventeenth Centuries*, Ann Arbor, 1950.
Webster	F. L. Lucas, ed., *The Complete Works of John Webster*, 4 vols., 1927.

4. *Journals*

ES	*English Studies*
JEGP	*Journal of English and Germanic Philology*
MLR	*Modern Language Review*
MP	*Modern Philology*
NQ	*Notes and Queries*
PMLA	*Publications of the Modern Language Association of America*
PQ	*Philological Quarterly*
RES	*Review of English Studies*
SB	*Studies in Bibliography*

ed.	editor
om.	omits
s.d.	stage direction
s.p.	speech prefix

INTRODUCTION

THE AUTHORS

THOMAS MIDDLETON was born in London in 1580. His father, 'a cittizen and Bricklayer', died when Thomas was only five years old and his school and university studies were pursued against a turbulent, litigious background of suits raised by his mother against his adventurer stepfather. He matriculated at Queen's College, Oxford, in 1598 but probably left without taking a degree, for early in 1601 he was reported to be 'heare in London daylie accompaninge the players'. These players were probably Philip Henslowe's Admiral's Men, for whom Middleton's earliest plays, now lost, were written. In 1602 or 1603 he married the sister of an actor in this company.

During the next ten years Middleton wrote many successful comedies and intrigues of town life. In such plays as *Michaelmas Term* (1605) and *A Trick to Catch the Old One* (*c.* 1606) he casts a sardonic eye on the seamy side of Jacobean London, using a clinical, realistic presentation of character and action to anatomize a society wholly motivated by greed. By 1609, however, the vogue for city comedy was yielding to a growing demand for the romantic drama of Beaumont and Fletcher. *Philaster* was performed in 1609 and *A King and No King* in 1611, and almost at once tragicomedy became 'the most popular dramatic form in England, and the term tragicomedy attained respectability for at least the next generation'.[1] Middleton responded to this demand, producing over the next decade a series of romantic tragicomedies such as *More Dissemblers Besides Women* (*c.* 1614) and *The Witch* (*c.* 1615) whose blending of sentiment and sensationalism shows the damaging effect of Fletcher's influence. Only in *A Fair Quarrel*, the finest of this group, is the influence firmly controlled, and in this play the psychology of character reaches a level of acuteness and complexity which the satiric point of view expressed in the earlier comedies had not permitted.

In 1613 Middleton began turning out pageants and entertainments for city occasions, averaging one a year until his death. His dramatic productivity continued undiminished, though the extra work was made possible by an increased proportion of collaborative writing, with Rowley as the most regular partner. In 1620 he was appointed City Chronologer, and to this period of public office belong *A Game*

[1] M. T. Herrick, *Tragicomedy: Its Origin and Development in Italy, France, and England*, Urbana, 1955, p. 260.

at Chess, a political satire which caused a furore and may have led to the author's imprisonment, and two great tragedies, *The Change-ling* (with Rowley) and *Women Beware Women*. He died in 1627.

William Rowley's parentage and early life are unknown, and when his name first appears it is as co-author of a mediocre adventure-play, *The Travels of the Three English Brothers* (1607).[2] Subsequent references show, however, that Rowley made a career primarily as an actor. From 1609 he was a member of the Duke of York's (later the Prince's) Men, acting in their daily performances and handling much of their business. By 1616 he had become leader of the company.

As an actor Rowley's special talent was the role of a fat clown. He is known, for example, to have taken the part of Plumporridge in Middleton's *Inner Temple Masque* and (after his move to the King's Men in 1623) the part of the Fat Bishop in *A Game at Chess*. In his own plays Rowley's policy was, not surprisingly, to include just such a character. The *dramatis personae* list of *All's Lost by Lust* announces that '*Jacques*, a simple clownish Gentleman' was 'person-ated by the Poet', and Rowley also both wrote and played the parts of Simplicity in *The World Tossed at Tennis* (with Middleton) and Bustopha in *The Maid in the Mill* (with Fletcher). The same policy seems to have been followed in *A Fair Quarrel*, where there is a clown, Chough, whose passion for wrestling also calls for an actor skilled in fat clown roles. Rowley certainly wrote the part; very probably he acted it as well.

As a playwright Rowley is generally neglected. Few would rank him, with Swinburne, as a 'very remarkable and original genius',[3] but he is equally undeserving of his current reputation as a col-laborating hack and a 'play doctor' who revamped greater dramatists' work. There is no evidence to connect him with the latter activity, and as a collaborator Rowley claims a share in some of the finest plays of the period (e.g., *The Witch of Edmonton* (with Dekker and Ford) and *The Changeling*). Another consequence of this neglect is the confusion besetting the Rowley canon. Only three plays, which have never been dated, or edited, satisfactorily, are usually admitted as his unaided work; of some fifty others he has at various times been named as part-author or reviser. Yet in contrast to modern scholars' marked lack of affection, Rowley was, according to Gerard Langbaine, 'beloved by those Great Men, *Shakespear*, *Fletcher*, and *Johnson*'.[4] He died in 1626.

[2] For a summary of findings on Rowley's life and career, see Bentley, II, 555–8; V, 1014–18.

[3] A. C. Swinburne, *The Age of Shakespeare*, 1908, p. 184.

[4] *An Account of the English Dramatic Poets*, 1691, p. 428.

DATE AND STAGE HISTORY

There are only two solid pieces of evidence which help to determine the probable date of composition: the use of Peter Lowe's *A Discourse of the Whole Art of Chirurgery* (1612), from which the dramatists pieced together the surgeon's speeches in IV, ii and V, i; and the appearance of Q1 in 1617 (the play was not entered in the Stationers' Register before publication). These fix definite limits, but evidence for a more specific date is less reliable. The strongest is the probability that the roaring-school scene (IV, i) was influenced by *Bartholomew Fair*, which would preclude composition before October 1614, when Jonson's comedy was performed (see H & S, IX, 245). In IV, iv of this play Knockem, Cutting, and company enjoy a game of 'vapours', the rules of which Jonson explains in a stage-direction:

> Here they continue their game of *vapours*, which is *non sense*. Euery man to oppose the last man that spoke: whether it concern'd him, or no.

Each bout is concluded by the participants taking a drink.[5] The activity has the same ritualistic character as the demonstration of roaring given in the 'school' (IV, i, 85ff.), both reduce language to 'non sense', and both 'conclude in wine'. There are other links between the two plays: *A Fair Quarrel* has a tobacco-man named 'Vapour', and *Bartholomew Fair* has Captain Whit, an Irish pimp like Captain Albo, and 'one *Puppy*, a Westerne man [i.e., a Cornishman] that's come to wrastle before my Lord *Maior*' (IV, iii, 113–15) who may have given the cue for Chough's portrayal as a Cornish wrestler. Both Middleton and Rowley knew the play—one had borrowed from it elsewhere, the other probably acted in it—and this makes imitation all the more likely.[6]

Historical considerations tend to corroborate a date of 1614 or later. The question of duelling debated in the main plot was highly topical between 1613 (especially after October, when James's first proclamation, *Prohibiting Reports of Duels*, was issued) and 1616. These years saw a sharp rise in the number of duels fought in

---

[5] H & S (X, 189) explain the game of vapours as Jonson's attempt 'to depict the contemporary roarer'.

[6] See C. R. Baskervill, 'Some Parallels to *Bartholomew Fair*', *MP*, 6 (1908–09), 116–19. As Jonson's play was acted by the Lady Elizabeth's Men when the Prince's were amalgamated with them (see Bentley, I, 198), Rowley must have assisted in its production and would have been the obvious choice to act Zeal-of-the-Land Busy.

England, laws passed to prevent them, and Star-Chamber trials of offenders (see note, p. 2). The burlesque of roaring in IV, i may have been similarly inspired, for roaring boys were particularly troublesome around 1615. Writing at the end of the year Sir Simonds D'Ewes complained that

> divers sects of vicious persons, under particular titles, pass unpunished or regarded, as the sect of Roaring Boys, Bravadoes, and such like.

According to D'Ewes it was impossible 'to walk the streets in safety after midnight'. This state of affairs may have prompted the satiric attack in *A Fair Quarrel*, just as it may have prompted two other attacks which appeared in 1615.[7] At any rate, the fact that *A Fair Quarrel* supplies *OED*'s earliest example of 'roaring' used as a noun in this sense, plus the fact that roarers had never been accorded such detailed treatment in any earlier play, is good evidence of the subject's topicality at the time of composition.

It is impossible to date the play more precisely than these general indications permit. The use of Bretnor's *New Almanac and Prognostication* at V, i, 122–7 is not authentic (indeed Bretnor nowhere employs the motto which Trimtram reads out), and the 'nineteenth of August' (V, i, 123), even if one can assume that it was the day of the play's first performance, does not exclude any year between 1613 and 1617 by falling on a Sunday. Finally, Sampson suggests that the reference to saltpetre-men at I, i, 243ff. was provoked by the granting of the earl of Worcester's saltpetre patent on 13 March 1617. This is unconvincing, since similar patents had been granted in 1607 and 1613, and resentment to the commission began in the previous century (see note). Until further evidence can be adduced, the received date of composition for the play, *c.* 1615–17, must stand.

IV, iv requires separate consideration. This second roaring scene did not appear in the original issue of Q1, but was printed and inserted into it sometime later in the same year, creating a second issue of the first edition of the play. The title-page was recast advertising 'new Additions of Mr. *Chaughs* and *Trimtrams* Roaring, and the Bauds Song', and the original title-leaf of Q1 cancelled. This change of plan could be accounted for in several ways; but the inserted scene's textual and bibliographical distinctness (see below, p. xliii), its complete detachability from the rest of the action, and its introduction of three new characters, all make it likely that the

[7] See J. O. Halliwell-Phillipps, ed., *The Autobiography and Correspondence of Sir Simonds D'Ewes*, 1845, II, 324; W. Goddard, *A Nest of Wasps*, 1615, sigs. D2r–D3r; Webster's addition of 'A Roaring Boy' to the sixth edition (1615) of Overbury's *Characters*.

decision to augment Q1 was taken because a stage-revival of the
play, for which Rowley had provided a new scene, had occurred
while Q1 was at press.[8] IV, iv, then, was probably written a year or
two later than the rest of Q1's text, in 1617. Its jocular self-adver-
tising reference to *A Fair Quarrel* as both new and popular (IV, iv,
13ff.) supports this, and suggests that the original version of the play
had proved successful enough to deserve a revival.

There is, indeed, ample evidence that *A Fair Quarrel* was a hit
with contemporary audiences, though the uncertain movements of
the Prince's Men between 1615 and 1617 make it impossible to
determine at which public theatre the play was first performed.
The familiarity of a reference to the play's roaring jargon in Webster
and Rowley's *A Cure for a Cuckold* (1624–25), IV, i, 120–4

> PETTIFOG. . . . This Informer comes into *Turnball-street* to a Victual-
> linghouse, and there falls in league with a Wench—
> COMPASS. A *Tweak*, or *Bronstrops*—I learnt that name in a Play

suggests that *A Fair Quarrel* had remained in active repertory, and
this is supported by its protection in 1639 as part of the repertory of
Beeston's Boys at the Phoenix. Reaction at Court was equally favour-
able: the mention of a performance 'before the King' on the title-
page of Q1, plus the occurrence of 'A ffaire Quarrell' in a list of
plays on waste-paper of the Revels Office, implies two court performances before 1620. Performances even continued into the
Restoration: in 1662 a certain Sir Edward Browne recorded payment
of '2sh. 6d.' to see 'The fair quarrell' 'At the Kings Armes Norwich'.[9]

SOURCES

The main plot is a striking example of Middleton's eclectic method of
composition. Materials were culled from a number of sources,
refashioned, and combined to create a powerful and original story.
The principal quarry was the subplot of Heywood's *A Woman Killed
with Kindness* (1603), which concerns a conflict between two friends

---

[8] Alternative, much less attractive, explanations are: (i) IV, iv was cut from
the original acting version for reasons of length (the play including IV, iv is
about 2,500 lines, which was no more than average); (ii) IV, iv formed part
of the printer's original MS but was excluded on aesthetic grounds either
by the publisher, John Trundle, or by the dramatists, and the decision later
reversed (a ballad publisher like Trundle can scarcely be credited with such
critical scrupulosity, and there is nothing to show that either author was so
closely involved in the printing of Q1).

[9] See Bentley, I, 330; IV, 867–8.

and their reconciliation when one falls in love with the other's sister and generously secures his release from prison by paying his debts. The brother expresses his sense of indebtedness by offering his sister to his former adversary.[10] In *A Fair Quarrel* the story is simplified to a bare framework of dispute—conflict—repentance—reconciliation, and in the process the relationships are changed: the sister exchanges brothers, becoming the sister of the man initially defeated. There is also a radical shift in emphasis: the original quarrel comes to assume central importance, while the gift-of-the-sister device is hurried in somewhat abruptly to supply the conventional twist of the tragicomic conclusion. (Note that the Colonel's sister is not heard of until III, i, 180, does not appear until IV, ii, and is never mentioned by Ager before his timely surrender to love-at-first-sight at IV, iii, 104.)

The fresh material which fills out this framework—Lady Ager's self-slander, Ager's dilemma, and the Colonel's remorse—illustrates Middleton's habit of repeating ideas and incidents from his earlier plays. Lady Ager's seven-year-old widow's vow (II, i, 109–10) has been kept for the same length of time by the Duchess of *More Dissemblers Besides Women* (*c.* 1614); and her desperate expedient to save her son is foreshadowed in *No Wit, No Help Like a Woman's* (1611), where Lady Twilight perjures herself for the same reason (though, as D. M. Holmes observes, 'Lady Ager's mother love is more impressive: her lie entails the sacrifice of her cherished reputation'[11]). Similarly, Ager's filial devotion recalls that of Fidelio in *The Phoenix* (*c.* 1604) who vows

> rather than the poor lady my mother should fall upon the common side of rumour to beggar her name, I would . . . in the stainless quarrel of her reputation, alter my shape forever.[12]

Hamlet has been suggested as an influence on the presentation of Ager's dilemma,[13] but a closer parallel is available in another Middleton play, *The Nice Valour* (*c.* 1615, with Fletcher). Here the

[10] The tale appears originally in an Italian *novella*, and twice in English prose translations before being dramatized by Heywood. There are, however, several points in which *A Fair Quarrel* agrees with Heywood's play against earlier versions. There are also some verbal parallels, and the incident of Lady Ager calling needlessly for a surgeon at IV, iii, 17–25 is clearly repeated from *A Woman Killed*, iii, 57–69 (ed. R. W. Van Fossen, 1961).

[11] *The Art of Thomas Middleton: A Critical Study*, 1970, p. 116.

[12] II, i, 7–12. Cf. Cleanthes of Middleton and Rowley's *The Old Law* (*c.* 1615–18), who is also placed in a crisis where preservation of self-esteem depends upon unswerving loyalty to a parent.

[13] By H. Jung, *Das Verhältnis Thomas Middletons zu Shakespere*, Leipzig, 1904, pp. 59–61. See notes to I, i, 30–1, II, i, 9, 28–9, 189, and below, p. xxv.

hero, a man with a scrupulous sense of honour, is anxious to redeem his reputation by fighting a duel, and is tormented by indecision and despair when circumstances prevent it. Finally, the Colonel's confession of guilt and repentance, together with the reading of his will and the nominee's horrified reaction to its contents (IV, ii, 40ff.), is modelled on Sir Walter Whorehound's similar admission in *A Chaste Maid in Cheapside* (1611–13), V, i.[14]

The surgeon's diagnoses (IV, ii, 4–32; V, i, 380–92) were pieced together from the first twenty pages of the sixth book, 'Of Wounds', of Peter Lowe's *A Discourse of the Whole Art of Chirurgery* (1612). Though often verbatim, the borrowing was not a matter of casual pilfering. The dramatists carefully sifted their material, making the surgeon's remarks internally consistent in respect of symptoms, diagnosis, and cure. The surgeon cares 'but little' for the oesophagal wound (IV, ii, 6), which Lowe accounts only 'dangerous', while he is much more worried by the wound in the midriff, which Lowe considers 'mortal'. The symptoms he observes—swelling, inflammation, convulsion, and the rest—are those which Lowe associates with a wound in this region, and the treatment that recommended by Lowe for a wound which is severe and difficult to heal.[15]

The subplot is a skilful redaction of *novella* IV, v of Cinthio's *Hecatommithi* (Venice, 1565). The rambling narrative was compressed without signs of haste or overcrowding to less than a thousand lines of verse and prose, the setting and characters anglicized, a new motive (the rich but foolish suitor) introduced, and changes made in the interests of dramatic effectiveness (Russell's stratagem in I, i and the interplay of veiled suggestions and mistaken intentions in the seduction scene (III, ii, 28ff.) are both additions to the source). The characters lose their nobility, and become stock types of the contemporary comedy of bourgeois life and manners. Fitzallen as the hard-done-by lover inevitably remains rather colourless, but Jane is transformed from the insipid, wilting creature of the *novella* to a characteristically spirited and resourceful comic heroine. Russell, a mere cipher in Cinthio, becomes a vigorous example of the devious, commercially-minded father who is willing to sacrifice his daughter's happiness to his plans for a profitable

[14] See R. V. Holdsworth, 'Middleton and Rowley's *A Fair Quarrel*: An Unnoticed Borrowing', *NQ*, 216 (1971), 25–7. Middleton's characters often undergo a sudden access of remorse; cf. *A Mad World, My Masters*, IV, i; *The Widow*, III, ii.

[15] See R. V. Holdsworth, 'The Medical Jargon in *A Fair Quarrel*', *RES*, 23 (1972), 448–54. G. R. Price, unaware of the source, mistakenly claims that the surgeon's treatment 'appears to be tentative and hardly correct' ('Medical Men in *A Faire Quarrell*', *Bulletin of the History of Medicine*, 24 (1950), 40).

match (his opening soliloquy, especially his emphasis on 'wit' at
I, i, 5, places him firmly in this tradition). Chough's role as the
fatuous suitor is equally traditional, and his and Trimtram's broad
combination of scurrility and slapstick mark them as typical Rowley
clowns.[16]

Further changes satisfy expectations of a neat and morally
palatable conclusion. In the *novella* the girl retains her pretence of
chastity, the child is raised as the physician's bastard by a foster
parent, and the physician murdered by the girl's family for his
supposed slander. Middleton and Rowley preserve the mood of
conventional domestic comedy by importing some familiar devices:
the lovers turn out to have been secretly married all along by a *de
praesenti* contract, and the tables are turned on the scheming Russell
in a fashion typical of the denouements of Middleton's comedies of
city life (in fact, for Cinthio's conclusion the authors substitute
virtually complete the resolution of Middleton's *The Family of Love*).
By the end all the characters have been chastened for their excesses:
Fitzallen has had a spell in prison, Jane has been forced to face her
troubles alone, Russell's double-dealing has rebounded upon him,
and the physician, now exposed and disgraced, appropriately retires
on a note of self-recrimination (V, i, 365).

The play's third line of action, concerning Chough's activities
as a would-be roarer, relies heavily on Jonson. The chief quarry was
The Alchemist (1610), from which various details of the plot involving
Kastril, another wealthy rustic (with a bird-name) who comes up to
London to learn 'the speech of the angry boys', are faithfully
repeated. *Bartholomew Fair* offered further suggestions (see above,
p.xiii), one of Adam Overdo's tirades in particular:

> Looke into any Angle o' the towne, (the Streights, or the *Bermuda's*)
> where the quarrelling lesson is read, and how doe they entertaine
> the time, but with bottle-ale, and tabacco? The Lecturer is o'
> one side and his Pupils o' the other; But the seconds are still bottle-
> ale, and tabacco, for which the Lecturer reads, and the Nouices
> pay. Thirty pound a week in bottle-ale! forty in tabacco! and ten
> more in Ale againe. Then for a sute to drinke in, so much, and (that
> being slauer'd) so much for another sute, and a third sute, and
> fourth sute! and still the bottle-ale slauereth, and the tabacco
> stinketh!   (II, vi, 76–86)

IV, i of *A Fair Quarrel* can be seen as an elaboration of this speech
in dramatic terms. The authors create a 'roaring-school', complete
with tutors, assistants, pupils (amongst whom 'the Nouices pay' for
drink and tobacco), syllabuses, and even a refectory service.

[16] Rowley was fond of master-servant doublings of clowns: cf. *Wit at Several
Weapons*, *The Changeling*, and *The Spanish Gypsy* (all with Middleton).

THE COLLABORATION

Most scholars, if they concede that 'two authors are in it, and in it as full, if not exactly equal, partners',[17] accept the division of the play made by Pauline G. Wiggin in 1897.[18] On the evidence of metrical tests (she estimates that Middleton's verse contains roughly twice as many feminine endings as Rowley's) supported by parallel passages in the dramatists' unaided plays, Miss Wiggin assigns the main plot including V, i, 379–431 to Middleton, and the rest of the play, including all of Act I, to Rowley. Miss Wiggin's evidence is questionable—parallel hunting as a guide to authorship is now largely discredited, and her metrical data were gathered from texts which had been extensively relined by nineteenth-century editors— yet her division seems broadly correct. It yields a pattern which is mechanically feasible (each collaborator taking one of the plots), it allocates to each dramatist parts of the play suited to his particular abilities and interests, and it agrees substantially with the divisions generally accepted for *The Changeling*, in which 'Rowley wrote the subplot and the opening and closing scenes of the play, and Middleton the remainder of the main plot'.[19] In fact, current supporters of Miss Wiggin challenge her division at only two points: Robb traces Middleton in 'the first two pages at least of I, i', and Cyrus Hoy, applying persuasively reliable linguistic tests, finds no sign of Middleton in Act V.[20]

The arguments of those who apportion the shares differently are uniformly unimpressive. Anthony Trollope and, independently, Havelock Ellis give the main plot to Rowley, but on no firmer 'evidence' than that of their own impressions.[21] Equally tenuous is the case presented by W. D. Dunkel, who demands 'Did Not Rowley Merely Revise Middleton?', finds that the answer is 'yes', and gives Middleton the whole of the play.[22] Dunkel's reasoning amounts to no more than a version of the game of parallels, and

[17] D. M. Robb, 'The Canon of William Rowley's Plays', *MLR*, 45 (1950), 130.
[18] *An Inquiry into the Authorship of the Middleton-Rowley Plays*, *Radcliffe College Monographs*, 9 (1897).

[19] N. W. Bawcutt, ed., *The Changeling*, 1958, p. xxxix.

[20] Robb, op. cit., 137; C. Hoy, 'The Shares of Fletcher and his Collaborators in the Beaumont and Fletcher Canon (V)', *SB*, 13 (1960), 85.

[21] See G. D. Johnson, 'Trollope's Note on Middleton and Rowley's *A Fair Quarrel*', *NQ*, 216 (1971), 27; Ellis, II, ix–xi.

[22] *PMLA*, 48 (1933), 799–805. 'Dunkel replies to his own question in the affirmative; it is the wrong answer' (S. Schoenbaum, *Internal Evidence and Elizabethan Dramatic Authorship*, 1966, p. 137).

played without much skill: for example, the appearance of a Dutch-speaking nurse in *A Fair Quarrel*, III, ii, and the fact that in IV, i of *A Chaste Maid* Tim Yellowhammer woos in Latin a Welshwoman who, mystified, replies in Welsh, can by only the most curiously vivid of imaginations be regarded as proof that Middleton wrote both scenes. Nevertheless, D. M. Holmes, in a recent book on Middleton, joins Dunkel in denying Rowley any share in *A Fair Quarrel*. His arguments, however, mark a regression even on Dunkel's vagaries: they range from the purely impressionistic ('the pervasiveness . . . of the idiom of Middleton's thought') to sheer fantasy (Rowley was merely a hack writer and was therefore allowed to act only as Middleton's 'pupil-assistant').[23]

Fortunately, it is now possible to corroborate Miss Wiggin's findings through the recent work done on Middleton and Rowley's linguistic practices as clues to their authorship.[24] A preference for certain colloquial contractions, individual methods of forming them, penchants for certain words (e.g., particular oaths)—these largely unconscious habits of style are less susceptible to variation than other, more literary features, such as metre and imagery, which are 'context-sensitive', may alter radically when one author collaborates with another, and do not permit reliable distinction between common authorship and imitation. Each dramatist's linguistic pattern contains contractional forms and other words which, since they never or hardly ever occur in that of the other, offer means of identification (in Middleton's case this can be verified not only from his printed plays but from the autograph and part-autograph MSS of *A Game at Chess*). When *A Fair Quarrel* is divided up according to the incidence of these usages in Q1 the divisions correspond strikingly to those established by Miss Wiggin, and incorporate Robb's and Hoy's adjustments:

	Middleton I, i, 1–93; II, i; III, i, iii; IV, ii, iii (substantially)	*Rowley* I, i, 93–424; II, ii; III, ii; IV, i, iv; V
I've	7	0
you'd	4	0
ha'	4	0
'em	6	0
a' (for *on* or *of*)	5	0

[23] op. cit., pp. 217–19.
[24] See Hoy, op. cit., 77–108; D. J. Lake, 'The *Pericles* Candidates—Heywood, Rowley, Wilkins', *NQ*, 215 (1970), 135–41; G. R. Price, 'The Early Editions of *A Trick to Catch the Old One*', *Library* (Fifth Series), 22 (1967), 210–12; P. B. Murray, *A Study of Cyril Tourneur*, Philadelphia, 1964, pp. 158–89.

	Middleton	*Rowley*
pish	2	0
hath	0	5
doth	0	2
'um	1	36
ye	2	5
tush	0	6

The only difficulty is IV, iii, where most of the evidence points to Middleton, but in which Rowley's *'um* (l. 55) and *ye* (l. 67, 'Yeare deare, and yeare good too: I thinke a that') also appear. Although it is possible to explain the two instances of *ye* as compositorial expansions of Middleton's *y'are* (note that Middleton's *a* occurs in the same line), this is unnecessary: it is only reasonable to expect that in the process of composition the collaborators read through one another's work, making occasional alterations. Scenes attributed above entirely to one author may well contain patches of writing by the other.

The transition to Rowley's linguistic pattern is regularly accompanied by the appearance of his familiar features of style: broad and obtrusively irrelevant puns (e.g., I, i, 120), as distinct from the pungent, ironical word-play of Middleton (cf. I, i, 17); 'cue-catching', the linking of speeches by the repetition of terminal words (e.g., I, i, 329–32; III, ii, 97–9); quibbles on place-names (e.g., II, ii, 191); and latinized diction and classical references (e.g., I, i, 96, 102, 173, 405). Middleton's fluent, flexible verse gives way to the rougher, staccato-like manner of his partner (e.g., III, ii, 118–40), and the characterization, lacking Middleton's sophisticated psychological approach, accords with Rowley's methods as outlined by Miss Wiggin:

> The motives of the characters are much simpler than is natural; they seem each to be moved by but one passion, of which they are somewhat conventionalized and extravagant exponents, and the passions are the universal ones of love, revenge, honor. Rowley makes no attempt to analyze conflicting emotions, or to exhibit both the strength and the weakness of his characters; the study of the subtler motives of human action had no attractions for him . . . His characters say too much; they foam at the mouth, beat each other and hurl invectives with astonishing freedom.[25]

[25] Wiggin, op. cit., pp. 15–18. For a full discussion of Rowley's style, see S. Schoenbaum, *Middleton's Tragedies: A Critical Study*, New York, 1955, pp. 203–17.

Typical of Rowley's approach to character is the disconcerting alacrity with which his heroines, when roused, will spit at the object of their disapproval (as Jane does at III, ii, 117).

These contrasting techniques which alternate through the play confirm that it is 'truly collaborative work' and that 'two authors are in it' as Robb maintains. They are also the foundation of Middleton and Rowley's unique success as a collaborating team. Middleton was able to devote his energies to the main plot, where the psychological tensions and the complex interactions of motive and behaviour called for his probing, analytical approach to character. In the subplot, which traditionally reflected the action and values of the main plot on a lower, less serious level, the tensions are more straightforward and more external. Here Rowley's vigorous, black-and-white mode of characterization was appropriate, and served to set the whole play on a firm moral basis. Rowley also took the roaring scenes, where he could exercise his flair for boisterous verbal and visual clowning. The result was a collaboration as balanced, as close, and as sympathetic as Middleton and Rowley later achieved in their greatest play, *The Changeling*.

THE PLAY

> Conscience is of greater price than Conceit.
> (James I, *Edict . . . against Private Combats*, 1614, p. 7.)

The theme of *A Fair Quarrel* is the nature of honour and the deceptiveness of reputation, and the play's three levels of action —main plot, subplot, and independent clown scenes—combine to expose the spuriousness of any external code of conduct. Each level is dominated by such a code; invariably its exponents are trapped, or trap themselves, into displays of folly and selfhood; and in the main plot and subplot—the third-level clowns being beyond redemption—a more genuine scheme of value finally triumphs. The physician in the subplot points the underlying moral (appropriately, since later he proves to be the very character who flouts it most brazenly):

> we are not born
> For ourselves only; self-love is a sin;
> But in our loving donatives to others
> Man's virtue best consists: love all begets;
> Without, all are adulterate and counterfeit.   (III, ii, 32–6)

Love, forgiveness, sympathy, and self-knowledge are the virtues celebrated by the play, and through them the tyranny of mechanical principle is finally rejected in favour of a notion of honour based on truth, charity, and tolerance.

Thematically, then, the play is a unity, but it would be wrong to view the characters of the main plot as simple schematic types. They are complex individuals, and Middleton probes their mixed motives and self-delusions with the same controlled, ironic detachment which distinguishes his treatment of character in such plays as *A Chaste Maid in Cheapside* and *Women Beware Women*. Like the characters of these plays, the Colonel, Ager, and Lady Ager are victims both of their own blindness and of the preoccupations of the society they inhabit. Not, in this case, a society motivated by lust and greed, but one committed to a fiercely sensitive cult of honour, beside which 'life—poor life . . . is but death and darkness' (III, i, 32–3). Like these characters too, they are subject to a system of ironies which governs the action, remorselessly exposing weakness.

Middleton's irony and detachment assert themselves immediately in Act I, in the quarrel over 'worth' between Ager and the Colonel. There is nothing sentimental or idealized in the conception here. Middleton was dramatizing accurately the almost pathologically intolerant attitude of the Jacobean gentry, familiar enough to be expounded in a contemporary treatise:

> Can any *Gentleman* suffer with patience his *Reputation* to be brought in question? Can he endure to be challenged in a publike place, and by that meanes incurre the opinion of a Coward? Can he put up disgrace without observance, or observing it, not *revenge* it, when his very *Honour* (the vital bloud of a *Gentleman*) is impeached?[26]

Middleton does not take sides. We watch while with fateful inevitability the Colonel's jealous care for reputation ('Life of the life') betrays him into a rage which blinds judgement, and Ager's conscientious scruples, vaunted by his friend at ll. 39–48, give way to smug self-righteousness and glib impertinence. (Critics who applaud Ager's 'cool reasonableness' here[27] might ponder the exchanges at ll. 84–93, and his taunting pretence of ignorance at l. 106.) The quarrel is patched up, but it breaks out again at the end of the act when, for a second time, the two men are obliged to take over a 'cause' not originally theirs. And this time the ironies cut deeper: though Ager claims 'Sir, you do wrong mine uncle', we are aware that the Colonel's accusations, violent as they are, are justified; Russell really is 'a blood-sucking churl'. R. H. Barker objects to

---

[26] R. Brathwaite, *The English Gentleman*, 1630, p. 43.
[27] e.g., S. Schoenbaum, 'Middleton's Tragicomedies', *MP*, 54 (1956–57), 16; Dorothy M. Farr, *Thomas Middleton and the Drama of Realism*, 1973, p. 39.

Ager's behaviour in the argument as 'priggish',[28] but this of course is the desired impression, for the conflict is not a crude one of hero versus villain, or of enlightened youth versus blinkered age. If the Colonel's insult, 'son of a whore', makes him seem 'a foul-mouthed fellow', Ager partly brings the insult on himself.

The point needs to be stressed, for since Charles Lamb's eloquent celebration of Ager's 'conscientious honour' and 'pious cowardice' many critics have seen him as a straightforward paragon of heroic excellence, 'thoroughly noble and lovable', the play's 'moral spokesmen', even 'the embodiment of male perfection'.[29] This is to commit the serious blunder of seeing Ager as he sees himself. Ager is not exempt from the main plot's testing pattern of ironies, nor is he a static character. He is changed by experience, and the change—like that which transforms Shakespeare's Isabella in *Measure for Measure* —is one from brittle, self-centred highmindedness to a warmer, more outgoing virtue.[30]

II, i lays bare the distortions of egoism in Ager's personality. Act I has ended with him facing, from the audience's point of view, a simple choice: given his scrupulous regard for truth, the patent falsity of the Colonel's aspersion (the dramatists have taken care to stress this at I, i, 357–60), and the fact that it was offered merely as the ritual insult for provoking a challenge, we might expect him either to fight the arranged duel without a second thought, or to dismiss the aspersion as meaningless and do nothing. In fact Ager's preoccupations impel him in quite a different direction. He opens Act II with an impassioned soliloquy, pitting his 'good opinion' of his mother's chastity against his 'judgement', based on the sin of Eve, that the Colonel's imputation of whoredom may well be true. But there is a deeper anxiety beneath this dilemma, and it is insistently self-regarding:

> I am . . .
> So careful of my eternity, which consists
> Of upright actions, that unless I knew
> It were a truth I stood for, any coward
> Might make my breast his footpace.   (II, i, 9–14)

[28] *Thomas Middleton*, New York, 1958, p. 109.

[29] Lamb, p. 136; Swinburne, op. cit., p. 163; Holmes, op. cit., p. 113; R. Levin, *The Multiple Plot in English Renaissance Drama*, 1971, p. 69.

[30] The parallel is illuminating, since the two plays share the same moral theme; with the physician's speech quoted above, compare *Measure for Measure*, I, i, 30–6: 'Thyself and thy belongings/Are not thine own so proper as to waste/Thyself upon thy virtues, they on thee/ . . . if our virtues/Did not go forth of us 'twere all alike/As if we had them not'.

Like Isabella, who has 'spirit to do anything that appears not foul in the truth of my spirit' (*Measure for Measure*, III, i, 202–3), Ager finds himself in a crisis where his ideal of truth can be maintained only by reducing other people to the status of objects. He probes his mother (even though ''tis too vild a question to demand indeed'), clears himself—deceitfully—when at first she vigorously asserts her innocence ('Nor did I fear your goodness, faithful madam'), and later, when she pretends that the charge is true in order to prevent the duel, greets the news of her incontinence in revealingly egocentric terms:

> Oh, were you so unhappy to be false,
> Both to yourself and me?—but to me chiefly:
> What a day's hope is here lost, and with it
> The joys of a just cause!   (II, i, 196–9)

To such depths of prevarication and self-deceit have Ager's scruples brought him.

But is this entirely adequate? Ager's tortured curiosity concerning his mother's chastity argues a further, darker motive—a subconscious Oedipean obsession. F. S. Boas hinted as much when he suggested that the main plot 'had its origins in the sexual mystifications which continually attracted [Middleton]',[31] and Samuel Schoenbaum took this suggestion further:

> In later plays ... Middleton's preoccupation makes possible psychological studies that reflect an almost Freudian awareness of how character may disintegrate before the implacable demands of sexuality. But in this instance it is a turn of the dramatist's mind, rather than his creation's, which stands revealed. For Captain Ager's strange doubts are never accounted for.[32]

Schoenbaum has pointed the way here, but to demand that the play supply prosaic explanations of Ager's obsession is to ignore the tact and subtlety with which Middleton treated sexual themes, particularly incest. (One thinks of the way Livia's repressed passion for her brother is delicately implied in *Women Beware Women*.) Some remarks by Ernest Jones, the psychologist, in *Hamlet and Oedipus*, show with what startling accuracy of insight Middleton has anticipated modern theory:

> When the attraction exercised by the mother is excessive it may exert a controlling influence over the boy's later destiny ... [he] may remain throughout life abnormally attached to his mother and unable to love any other woman ... The underlying theme [of

[31] *An Introduction to Stuart Drama*, 1946, p. 237.
[32] Schoenbaum, 'Middleton's Tragicomedies', 17.

Hamlet's dilemma] relates ultimately to the splitting of the mother image which the infantile unconscious effects into two opposite pictures: one of a virginal Madonna, an inaccessible saint towards whom all sensual approaches are unthinkable, and the other of a sensual creature accessible to everyone ... Misogyny, as in the play, is the inevitable result ... there is thus produced the picture of apparently causeless inhibition which is so inexplicable both to Hamlet and to readers of the play. This paralysis arises, however, not from physical or moral cowardice, but from that intellectual cowardice, that reluctance to dare the exploration of the inmost soul, which Hamlet shares with the rest of the human race. 'Thus conscience does make cowards of us all'.[33]

No clinical 'explanation' could do justice to the passionate yet fragile intimacy between mother and son which Middleton has captured in *A Fair Quarrel*; yet the relevance of these comments is clear. Ager is the recipient of excessive maternal affection (this is continually stressed; cf. I, i, 28, 34–5; II, i, 149; III, iii, 22; IV, iii, 16–31), he is hostile to women (cf. II, i, 28–9; IV, iii, 102–3), and his behaviour implies precisely the inhibitions and conflicts which Jones discusses (notice especially at II, i, 30–1 the disguised self-contradiction in 'Certain she's good; /There only wants but my assurance in't'). At one point, moreover, Jones's remarks on 'two opposite pictures' are echoed with striking literalness (IV, iii, 4–11). Middleton showed continual interest in the mother-son relationship, but in no other play did he invest it with such complexity of feeling, or explore its sexual nuances so searchingly. Barker's comparison with Ibsen's *Ghosts* is no more than just.[34]

In the subplot scene which follows II, i there are some lines clearly meant as an oblique criticism of Ager's conduct:

> Lord, what plain questions you make problems of!
> Your art is such a regular highway
> That, put you out of it, and you are lost.   (II, ii, 22–4)

The tone is mocking but genial, and this is appropriate, for despite its serious mood the main plot is a comedy, concerned with the

[33] 1949, pp. 77, 86, 91. It is interesting to compare Schoenbaum's objection to T. S. Eliot's well-known complaint that Hamlet's emotion concerning his mother's guilt is 'in *excess* of the facts as they appear'.

[34] Barker, op. cit., pp. 108–10. Cf. this relationship in *The Phoenix*, *Michaelmas Term*, *No Wit No Help*, *Women Beware Women*, and *Father Hubburd's Tales* (Bullen, VII, 102). Middleton's interest clearly owes much to the unhappy events of his childhood; relevant articles are J. B. Brooks, 'Middleton's Stepfather and the Captain of *The Phoenix*', *NQ*, 206 (1961), 382–4, and Marilyn L. Williamson, 'Middleton's Workmanship and the Authorship of *The Puritan*', *NQ*, 202 (1957), 50–1 (on the hasty widow theme).

correction of error and folly and not with retribution for evil or sin. Ager is not a 'bad' character, any more than the Colonel. Both are basically self-ignorant, and both find self-knowledge through the crisis their self-ignorance has caused.

Ager's journey to self-awareness can be viewed in terms of a struggle between inner impulse and outward principle, between the spontaneous urgings of love and sympathy and the inflexible demands which the 'noble code' of his society lays on conduct. In III, i, robbed of his cause, Ager can let his deepest feelings speak:

> Thousands have made a less wrong reach to hell,
> Ay, and rejoiced in his most endless vengeance—
> A miserable triumph, though a just one.
> But when I call to memory our long friendship,
> Methinks it cannot be too great a wrong
> That then I should not pardon.   (III, i, 76–81)

Vengeance would be both 'just' and 'miserable' because exacted at the expense of charity. But on this occasion Ager's insight is short-lived. Another cause immediately presents itself in the Colonel's second insult, 'coward', and at once the claims of 'just manhood' and 'anger' reassert themselves. Ager fights, defeats his adversary, and rejoices in just such a 'miserable triumph' as he had previously repudiated:

> Truth never fails her servant, sir, nor leaves him
> With the day's shame upon him.   (III, i, 165–6)

Truth has indeed won in one sense (it is not true that Ager is a coward); but in another—in terms of Ager's growth to self-knowledge —it has been defeated. The inner promptings of 'mildness,/Peace, constant amity, and calm forgiveness' (III, i, 70–1) have paid the price of a code which sets pride above humility.[35]

In IV, iii the debt is reversed. Through an example of self-sacrifice set by the Colonel's sister, Ager finally sees his own failings and acknowledges a more generous, more human ideal of truth and virtue. It is essential to view this scene as a whole, although Schoenbaum regards its conclusion, and what follows in Act V, as a disastrous capitulation to the exigencies of the tragicomic formula:

> the play does not end with Lady Ager's last speech [IV, iii, 84–90]. Instead Middleton goes on to show how the Colonel repents and recovers and is reconciled with the Captain. Thus the tension which gives the central scenes their power is relieved, and the unsparing

[35] Referring, presumably, to this scene, Miss M. C. Bradbrook accuses the play of being 'remarkably inconsistent' in its attitude to the duelling code (*The Growth and Structure of Elizabethan Comedy*, 1955, p. 238); but the inconsistency is plainly Ager's, not Middleton's.

view of life that narrative and characterization have embodied is destroyed. The conventions, which Middleton did so much to transform, have triumphed in the end.[36]

Psychologically, the end of this scene is certainly weak: stock comic motifs like 'the gift of the sister' and love-at-first-sight jar discordantly with the realistic, exploratory view of character which the main plot encourages. Structurally, however, it is fully functional, for it combines with the rest of IV, iii to establish a carefully planned, thematic contrast with an earlier scene, II, i. The two scenes strike an obvious narrative balance (one leads Ager into his dilemma, the other leads him out of it), and their construction is identical, each following the same three stages: an anguished soliloquy by Ager; an intense, emotional encounter between Ager and his mother; a further, equally emotional encounter between Ager and a character (or pair of characters) who enters after Lady Ager has left. These formal resemblances underscore some crucial points of difference. In II, i Lady Ager falsely confesses incontinence to deprive Ager of his cause; in IV, iii she truthfully announces her chastity and thus—unintentionally—restores it. Ager now seems confirmed in the self-glorying ideals which the events of II, i had turned against him (cf. IV, iii, 72–4), but more ironic contrasts follow. In II, i Ager's friends—orthodox, unthinking members of 'the fellowship of honour'—enter to conduct him to his duel with the Colonel, and he feigns respect for his opponent as an excuse not to fight (II, i, 235–6). At the equivalent point in IV, iii it is the Colonel's sister who enters, coming from her brother to offer herself in marriage to Ager as a sign of repentance. Ager again voices respect for the Colonel, but this time he is deeply sincere, and as a result he is at last able to perceive the 'slow perfection' of his own virtue (IV, iii, 115–17, 123–5). The final twist occurs at the end of the scene, when Ager accepts the Colonel's sister as his bride. This makes a suitably deflationary comment on his pompous lecture to the Colonel in Act I—

> Virginity and marriage are both worthy,
> And the positive purity there are some
> Have made the nobler   (I, i, 85–7)

—but it also completes the series of contrasts with II, i, for this scene had ended with a pious prayer from Ager's friends concerning his cowardice:

> Pardon this traitorous slumber, clogged with evils:
> Give captains rather wives than such tame devils!
>
>   (II, i, 251–2)

---

[36] Schoenbaum, 'Middleton's Tragicomedies', 18.

Their request has ironically been granted, and the way to reconciliation is now clear. It is achieved without loss of tension. On the
contrary, Ager's humble admission to his former enemy at the end of
the play—

> You have a goodness
> Has put me past my answers; you may speak
> What you please now, I must be silent ever   (V, i, 424–6)

—is charged with significance, for it refers us back to the original
quarrel, and sets foregiveness above the ritual of insults and chal-
lenges. 'Love all begets;/Without, all are adulterate and counterfeit'.

As Ager is no simple hero, the Colonel is far from being merely
'the villain . . . whose main function is to force the hero into his
dilemma'.[37] The key to his folly, however, is less complex. 'Spleen
and rage abuses him' (II, i, 237), and this weakness is repeatedly
stressed; explicitly (e.g., II, i, 72; III, i, 121, 175; IV, ii, 98),
through imagery of storms and tempests (I, i, 137–8, 151, 394; III,
i, 67–9), and in his ranting assertion at I, i, 163 that he would
challenge even his own father to maintain his honour (Ager's filial
shortcomings are more insidious). But the Colonel's blustering
self-importance does not characterize the inner man. Several well-
observed touches imply an essential generosity of spirit (I, i, 188–91;
II, i, 139; III, i, 127), and thus, when the façade is punctured and
remorse follows, there is no suggestion of crude tragicomic contri-
vance; the impression of a sudden, painful uprush of guilt and
conscience in a basically virtuous nature is wholly convincing.

In short, the Colonel's progress from arrogance to humility
directly parallels Ager's. The traumas of both men are self-invited
—the Colonel realizes 'I pursued my ruin' (III, i, 176), just as Ager
'will . . . needs tempt a ruin that avoids [him]' (IV, iii, 90)—and
each reaches the same maturity of insight, Ager's 'Truth' becoming
tempered with charity and tolerance, and the Colonel learning that
the only reputation of real value is that earned by 'a true man in
deed' (IV, ii, 52). These verbal links are not fortuitous. Ager and
the Colonel are constantly echoing one another's thoughts and turns
of phrase, and the impression this creates of a deep, unconscious
affinity between them—deeper than their enmity or the code which
sustains it—is one of the main plot's finest psychological strokes.[38]
As reconciliation approaches the echoes multiply, until the final
poignant moment at V, i, 396–411 when the two men confront one

[37] Levin, op. cit., p. 69.
[38] Cf. II, i, 5–7, III, i, 178–9; III, i, 89, 148; III, i, 182–3, IV, iii, 123–5;
IV, ii, 92–3, IV, iii, 8–9; IV, ii, 116, IV, iii, 3.

another across the stage and, speaking aside to their friends, declare their contrition in precisely similar terms (note especially the repetition of 'shame' and 'confounds'). There is no triumph of the conventions here; the requirements of character and theme have alike been met.

While Middleton's main plot examines the military-aristocratic values of 'the field', Rowley's subplot contrasts those of 'the city' (cf. I, i, 295–6)—the world of the busily acquisitive middle class. Not pride but avarice is the besetting sin of this society, for its chief preoccupations are money and the prestige money bestows. Its code of honour is shaped accordingly. Outward respectability becomes all-important—

> a good name's dear,
> And indeed more esteemed than our actions,
> By which we should deserve it   (III, ii, 162–4)

—since honour is measured solely by riches:

> Honour and attendance, these will bring thee health;
> And the way to 'em is to climb by wealth.   (I, i, 423–4)

In consequence, virtue becomes degraded to the level of a vendible commodity; even duty, loyalty, and love have their 'price'.[39]

The subplot's most vigorous, and most engaging, exponent of this philosophy is Russell. It is he who opens the play, announcing himself in a gloating, self-congratulatory soliloquy as a cynical sharper who regards life as a financial enterprise and other people as commercial objects. Jane, his daughter, is a piece of fragile merchandise, 'a mere cupboard of glasses', and as a prospective son-in-law Fitzallen has no 'worth' because he has no money. Russell has cunning, resourcefulness, and complete lack of principle to help him realize his paternal plans ('to cast her upon riches'), but he is subject to the same law of ironic discomfiture which operates in the main plot. Thus, Russell, the champion of 'wit', outwits himself. His guise, both to dispose of Fitzallen and to entice his own candidate for the marriage, 'a lad of thousands', is that of the trustingly complacent father, a guise of 'easy confidence' (cf. I, i, 15–19; II, ii, 146–8); and he is finally outmanoeuvred by precisely the eventuality this false pose would have invited had it been genuine. For, unknown to him, Jane is pregnant, the exchange value of her virginity has been debased from the beginning: 'All is not gold that glistereth in bed'

[39] Cf. I, i, 368; III, ii, 6, 110; also I, i, 245, 275, 411; III, ii, 15–24; IV, i, 7–8; V, i, 330–5.

(V, i, 305). Like the sharpers of Middleton's city comedies, 'the old man has gulled himself finely' (V, i, 371).[40]

Though pregnant, Jane is also secretly betrothed; and her courageous determination to remain true to this 'jugal knot', despite the risk of losing outward reputation, marks the subplot's most emphatic rejection of the specious code of honour which the driving mercenariness of her world promotes. Her dilemma is posed in III, ii, where she attempts to reward the physician who has discreetly assisted at the birth of her child. As he is unaware of her marriage-contract, she begins by thanking him as though she too cared only for appearances:

> you preserve my name,
> Which I had forfeited to shame and scorn . . .
> Your secrecy keeps me in the state of woman;
> For else what husband would choose me his wife,
> Knowing the honour of a bride were lost?   (III, ii, 48–58)

But Jane is jolted out of her pose when the physician promptly turns this notion of honour against her. For he, it becomes clear, is another 'outside of a man' who, like Russell, views Jane as an expensive sexual object. Jane's 'name'—her 'honour' in this sense—will be safe, provided she yield him the pleasure of her body (this, he declares, is his 'price', she will then be his 'creditress'), and he sends on his sister to make the consequences of refusal clear:

> Your reputation lies at his mercy,
> Your fault dwells in his breast; say he throw it out,
> It will be known; how are you then undone!
> Think on't, your good name; and they are not to be sold
> In every market.   (III, ii, 158–62)

But Jane's honour is 'above the quantity of price' (cf. III, ii, 6). She retains her integrity, and, when the physician again threatens exposure in order to ruin her imminent forced marriage to Chough, rejects both his and Russell's plans in a ringing denunciation of their code of false appearances:

> I'll rather bear the brand of all that's past
> In capital characters upon my brow,
> Than think to be thy whore or marry him.   (V, i, 23–5)

Disaster seems inevitable, but at this point Rowley introduces a neatly connected series of plots, counterplots, mistakes, and decep-

---

[40] Cf. the final line of *A Trick to Catch the Old One:* 'Who seem most crafty prove oft times most fools', and note the way Russell equivocates at his own expense at I, i, 253–5 and II, ii, 143. Cf. also III, i, 88–9: 'He must expect the same return again/Whose venture is deceitful'.

tions which secure a happy outcome. Their originator is, ironically, the physician, whose attempts to carry out his threat consistently misfire. Earlier, promising to save Jane's reputation, he had boasted his allegiance to a frankly specious view of virtue:

> we physicians are the truest
> Alchemists, that from the ore and dross of sin
> Can new distil a maidenhead again.   (II, ii, 130–2)

Now, seeking to ruin her, he employs the same metaphor to feign allegiance to a more genuine code:

> Your bride that may be has not that portion
> That a bride should have . . .
> I do not speak of rubbish, dross, and ore,
> But the refined metal, honour, sir.   (V, i, 81–5)

The argument fails dismally. The physician's mercenary values are also the bridegroom's; he meets only wondering incomprehension:

> Why, sir, she has a thousand and a better penny . . . What she wants in honour shall be made up in worship, sir; money will purchase both.   (V, i, 83–7)

Though his aid is eventually enlisted, Chough, the 'rich simplicity', proves hardly an ideal accomplice. Nor does the Dutch nurse, who, produced by the physician to clinch the question of Jane's motherhood, faithfully repeats what he has earlier told her—that he himself is the father of the child (V, i, 258). The physician's final defeat is equally ironic. Having tormented Jane with the threat of public shame ('I will defame thee ever . . . Bring thee to public penance'), he finds, his viciousness uncovered, that this is the very fate which overtakes him—and more crushingly, since he loses both outward and self-respect:

> I am ashamed.
>   Shame to amendment then.   (V, i, 365)

The physician's repentance redeems him for the subplot's comic finale, and this, in the traditional form of a wedding, is readily achieved, for the ceremony is prepared and all that is required is a substitution of bridegrooms. Fitzallen is thus reunited with Jane, and even the money-minded Russell, outsmarted financially, learns to find consolation in 'a father's love'.

The clown scenes parody the action of main plot and subplot, sharpening the play's indictment of their mechanical codes. In the roaring-school, for example, which is run by the Colonel's friend and attended by Chough because he wishes to 'proceed in the reputation of gallantry' (II, ii, 204), the ritual of duelling is debased to

* *

a fantastic, elaborately meaningless game, involving extravagant slanging-matches but no bloodshed:

> in our practice we grow to a quarrel, then there must be wine ready to make all friends—for that's the end of roaring, 'tis valiant, but harmless.   (IV, i, 53–6)

A Jacobean audience would have been quick to spot the parody, for the school, with its formal lessons, its tutors, assistants, and pupils, bears a strong if grotesque resemblance to the London fencing-schools (mentioned by Chough at II, ii, 202), which taught the nicer points of duelling etiquette. Middleton himself denounces these institutions in *The Peacemaker*:

> the compounding of quarrels is grown to a trade, and . . . there be some counsel learned of duels, that teach young gentlemen when they are beforehand and when behindhand, and thereby incense and incite them to the duel, and make an art of it.[41]

The effect of making a 'trade' and an 'art' of roaring is a levelling one: roaring and duelling become simply different versions of the same inane exercise.

Some specific parallels press the parody home. Thus, the dispute over worth and rank between Ager and the Colonel in Act I is repeated in Chough's mock quarrel in the school on the same theme ('Wilt thou not yield precedency?' etc.), and the Colonel's ritual insult, 'son of a whore', is echoed in the more elaborate but no less vacuous insults of the roarers ('I say thy mother is a calicut, a panagron, a duplar, and a sindicus').[42] IV, iv, where Chough and Trimtram practise their roaring on the uninitiated, has a similar function. In I, i and II, i Captain Ager is obliged by the duelling code to pretend that the Colonel's purely formal imputation of whoredom is sincerely meant, and Lady Ager, who is actually chaste, pretends that it is true. IV, iv apes this situation, criticizing its charade-like quality through some nightmarish distortions: here the pimp, 'Captain' Albo (his name encourages the comparison), must defend the 'fame' of his charges, the real whores Meg and

---

[41] Bullen, VIII, 337–8. Two memorable burlesques of quarrelling 'in print by the book' can be found in *As You Like It*, V, iv, 66–97 and *Romeo and Juliet*, II, iv, 20–37.

[42] A Jacobean audience would have been quick to notice this parallel also, since 'son of a whore' was itself a favourite insult with roaring boys. Kastril uses it in *The Alchemist*, IV, vii, 5, and cf. Field's *Amends for Ladies*, V, ii, 272–5: 'Dam-me, yee are all the sonne of a whoore, and ye lie, and I will make it good with my sword, this is cal'd Roaring father' (W. Peery, ed., *The Plays of Nathan Field*, Austin, 1950).

Priss, against equally formal imputations which, though patently true, both they and he pretend are false.

Chough's clownish vulgarity has the same reductive effect on the materialistic values of the subplot. His view of Jane is even more frankly mercenary than Russell's ('if my father-in-law gives me a good dowry with his daughter, I shall hold up my head well enough'), and even more brutally physical than the physician's ('Oh that thou didst but love wrestling!'); while some of his obscene puns contrive to combine both views at once ('Take her e'en to you with all her moveables'). 'Honour', too, Chough reduces to these terms: he equates it either with money (V, i, 86–7), or with the rules of a wrestling-bout (II, ii, 163).

Yet the clowns' antics serve as more than a simple parodic counterweight to the posturings and pretensions of the major characters. From one point of view, the sheer lunatic arbitrariness of their banter and jargon sets them apart as alien invaders from the world of farce; but from another, the verbal anarchy they let loose is only the ultimate stage of a process illustrated throughout the play: a process in which language, when it is no longer used as a vehicle of truth, breaks down, and meaningful communication is stifled, mutilated, and finally destroyed. 'Wheresoever manners, and fashions are corrupted', Jonson observes,

> Language is . . . *Speech* is the only benefit man hath to expresse his excellencie of mind above other creatures. It is the Instrument of *Society* . . . In all speech, words and sense are as the body, and the soule. The sense is as the life and soule of Language, without which all words are dead . . . *Language* most shewes a man: speake that I may see thee.[43]

A Fair Quarrel is full of seemers and deceivers, people concerned not to be 'seen' (even Lady Ager (II, i, 149ff.) and Anne (III, ii, 141ff.) can be included in this category). In consequence, speech becomes not the instrument of society, but of isolation; 'language' as well as 'manners' is corrupted.

Symptoms of this corruption abound. The most blatant, of course, is the 'damnable noise' of roaring, with its several dialects, 'the Sclavonian, Parthamenian, Barmeothian, Tyburnian, Wappinganian, or the modern Londonian'; but this is only one of many private languages which baffle communication in the play. Elsewhere the jargons of duelling, fencing, medicine, wrestling, tobacco-selling, the underworld cant of pimps and prostitutes, the pidgin Dutch of the nurse, all thicken the smokescreen of talk. (Even the Colonel's tirade at I, i, 336–42 may be cited here; it is closer to the 'roaring

---

[43] *Timber, or Discoveries* 1641 (H & S, VIII, 593, 620–1, 625).

curses' in IV, iv than to significant speech.) Verbal duplicity, too, is all-pervasive. The crudest example is Chough's 'trick' at V, i, 301ff., where, having promised not to 'speak a word' about Jane's pregnancy, he sings the information instead of saying it; but the equivocations of Ager (II, i, 35ff.), Jane (II, ii, 5ff.), the physician (III, ii, 42ff.), and Russell (continually) differ only in the degree of their sophistication.[44]

The effect of all this mystification and double-talk is to widen the play's definition of honour to include not only integrity, moral truth, but also literal truth and plain speaking. The hollowness and deceptiveness of mere words is a persistent theme. Thus, Ager, in his moment of insight in Act III, realizes that to kill the Colonel would be to revenge nothing more than 'a poor hasty syllable or two' (III, i, 82), and the Colonel's sister invokes a similar idea when she dismisses the academic claptrap of the surgeon:

> What thankless pains does the tongue often take
> To make the whole man most ridiculous!
>   . . . What a precious good
> May be delivered sweetly in few words,
> And what a mount of nothing has he cast forth!
>
>   (IV, ii, 33–8)

Elsewhere the theme is carried on implicitly: on the level of action, in the way that pairs of speakers are constantly wrestling with one another (as Chough, literally, wrestles), striving to penetrate the screen of language and link words with thoughts, motives, and actions; on the verbal level, in the way that various key terms, all to do with communication, regularly occur. *Tongue,* for example, appears ten times, *plain* and *plainly* eleven, *understand* and *understanding* twelve. *Speak* is even more frequent. It occurs nearly forty times, reaching a refrain-like climax in Act V in the word-combat fought between Chough, the physician, and Russell:

> I would speak with your master, sir . . .
> Let me speak with him ere he go to church . . .
> Who's that would speak with me?
>   None but a friend, sir;
> I would speak with you.
> Why, sir, and I dare speak with any man under the universe . . .
> All that I speak, sir, is in love to you . . .
> I do not speak of rubbish, dross, and ore . . .
>   what I speak

[44] Note that a current sense of *chough*, besides 'Cornish seabird' and 'simpleton', was 'prattler, chatterer'; cf. *All's Well that Ends Well*, IV, i, 21–2: 'chough's language, gabble enough, and good enough'.

My life shall maintain . . .
put up and speak freely . . .
          mistake me not; I do not speak
To break the contract of united hearts . . .
entreat my father-in-law that might have been to come and speak
with me . . .
Pray you speak to my understanding, sir . . .
Good sir, speak English to me.   (V, i, 42–157)

Finally, there is the word *word* itself. This, too, echoes up and
down the play, and in such a way that words seem to become not so
much symbols of meaning as tangible, potentially dangerous objects
with an anarchic life of their own. For example:

          Words did pass
Which I was bound to answer . . .
What words, sir, and of whom?   (I, i, 59–64)

Can words beget swords and bring 'em forth?   (I, i, 95)

No words can move this noble soldier's sword   (I, i, 174)

          give 'em very good words
To save my ground unravished, unbroke up   (I, i, 251–2)

          speak, sir . . .
The words, whate'er they were   (II, i, 83–5)

Choose your own word; I know you're sorry for't   (III, i, 97)

the gentlemen seem to give us very good words.
Good words? ay, if you could understand 'em; the words cost
twenty pound   (IV, iv, 71–4)

What's the word? . . .
The word is, sir, 'There's a hole in her coat'   (V, i, 126–7)

You'll stand to your words, sir?   (V, i, 137)

          give not too much belief
To his wild words   (V, i, 216–17)

Though the clowns continue jabbering happily into Act V, the
tyranny of words begins to decline in III, ii when Jane and Anne—
the first characters to do so—achieve firm and genuine communication ('Do you speak your soul?—By my soul do I'). And later this is
matched in the main plot, by a similar growth of understanding
between the repentant Colonel and his sister ('I know if you dare
swear, I may believe'). Act V sees further progress. Ager tersely

deflates the still gabbling surgeon (V, i, 385), and Jane, who in
II, ii had reduced truth to a mere counter in the game of quibbles
('I cannot tell the truth where my grief lies'), makes an honest
confession to her father:

> Come, tell truth 'twixt ourselves; here's none but friends . . .
> The truth, and thereby try my love abundant . . .
> JANE
> Then it's true, sir, I have a child.   (V, i, 231–6)

Truth, literal and moral, is finally reinstated in both plots, and in
the same way. Russell brushes aside the inane back-chat of Chough
and Trimtram—

> now no more words on't
> Till we be set at dinner   (V, i, 375–6)

—just as Ager cuts through the obfuscations of language which
estranged him from the Colonel:

> you may speak
> What you please now, I must be silent ever.   (V, i, 425–6)

Compared to the lubricity of words, the innocence of silence is
unimpeachable.

The play's narrative and verbal structures reinforce its unity of
theme.[45] After Act I, which skilfully launches the main and subplots
through a causally dependent series of incidents, the three lines of
action develop independently and do not meet again until the close
of the play. They are co-ordinated throughout, however, by a net-
work of parallels linking situations and characters. Thus, each plot
hinges on a 'fair quarrel' over the same question, a woman's chastity,
and each establishes the same three-cornered grouping of insulter
(the Colonel, the physician, Chough), insulted (Lady Ager, Jane,
Meg and Priss), and defender (Ager, Russell, Albo). In the main plot
and subplot this analogical technique is taken further. Both plots
focus on the dilemma of a child (Ager, Jane) whose 'honour' is
jeopardized by the misguided action of a parent (Lady Ager,
Russell), and who is finally rescued by the intervention of the
insulter's sister (the Colonel's sister, Anne). The same planned
intricacy characterizes the play's language. As the three plots are
arranged in descending order on the social scale, so each has its own
distinctive and appropriate strand of imagery (respectively, religious,
financial, and smuttily sexual), and its own distinctive tone: the
verse of the main plot is formal and heightened, abounding in

---

[45] I am partly indebted to Levin here (op. cit., pp. 66ff.), though I do not
agree with his general view of the play.

abstractions; that of the subplot relaxed and factual; while in the clown scenes the norm descends to doggerel rhyme in the songs and plain prose in the dialogue. At the same time, the thematic equivalence of the three plots is emphasized by the insistent, ubiquitous repetition of many important individual words. *Honour*, *fame*, *name*, *reputation*, *truth*, *false*, *shame*, and *sin* are the most obvious examples, but the dramatists also exploit the rich variety of senses in *fair* (this alone occurs twenty-six times), *dear*, *worth*, *good*, *goodness*, *perfect*, and *perfection*.

Middleton's verse-style must also be mentioned. This, in II, i, III, i, and IV, iii especially, has the same stark forcefulness of statement, the same 'pregnant simplicity' of cadence, which critics have so often praised in *The Changeling*.[46] For example:

> Now what's the friendly fear that fights within me,
> Should his brave noble fury undertake
> A cause that were unjust in our defence,
> And so to lose him everlastingly
> In that dark depth where all bad quarrels sink,
> Never to rise again. What pity 'twere
> First to die here, and never to die there!   (II, i, 76–82)

>   Quench, my spirit,
> And out with honour's flaming lights within thee!
> Be dark and dead to all respects of manhood!
> I never shall have use of valour more.   (II, i, 204–7)

There is no striving after effect here. The vocabulary is commonplace, the metaphor, apart from a few striking touches ('friendly fear', 'honour's flaming lights'), sparse and subdued. It is, rather, the directness and lucidity of these lines which gives them their power, assisted, unobtrusively, by alliteration, assonance, and a subtle, flexible use of rhythm and phrasing (notice, for example, the way sound enacts sense in 'In that . . . again'). Middleton's verse in *A Fair Quarrel* may, as Arthur Symons claims, 'shine like fire and cut like steel';[47] but it is true also that verbal pyrotechnics are avoided.

The play has, admittedly, its flaws. Rowley's two long clown scenes are awkwardly situated, coming close together in Act IV while the subplot is left suspended. The subplot itself contains another weakness: the character of Fitzallen. Fitzallen combines two basically opposed types, the hard-done-by lover and the penniless, dowry-hunting gallant, and it is never made clear to which camp

---

[46] e.g., M. C. Bradbrook, *Themes and Conventions of Elizabethan Tragedy*, 1935, pp. 217, 238–9; Bawcutt, op. cit., pp. lx–lxii.

[47] 'Middleton and Rowley', *The Cambridge History of English Literature* 15 vols., 1907–27, VI, 74.

he actually belongs; whether, in other words, Russell's charges of beggary have any substance. A third, more serious fault appears in the main plot. Lady Ager, as Schoenbaum observes, is 'yet another victim of the irony which overtakes weakness', since 'it never occurs to her that her "goodness" is really an excess of mother love'.[48] (At II, ii, 189 the subplot passes its own oblique, and typically oversimplified, comment here: 'domination is a woman's heaven'.) But after her poignant lines at IV, iii, 84–90, which Schoenbaum believes are 'perhaps the crucial speech of the play', Lady Ager drops out of the action, making only a mute, evidently perfunctory, appearance in Act V. Thus she alone is omitted from the redemptive process which educates the other characters to self-knowledge and reconciliation. Such defects, however, are minor. *A Fair Quarrel* remains one of the finest tragicomedies, and one of the very few first-rate collaborate plays, in English. We might even take a lesson from the roaring tutor:

Well, well, I will not see small faults. (IV, i, 146)

NOTE ON THE TEXT

Q1, the only authoritative text of the play, was published by John Trundle in 1617 and sold at Christ Church Gate by Edward Wright. The printer for some reason omitted to identify himself on the title-page, but G. R. Price[49] has shown conclusively from the evidence of wood-block ornaments that he was George Eld, a major Jacobean printer with a staff used to dealing with plays. (In all some forty came off his presses, including several of Middleton's, as well as the quartos of *Troilus and Cressida, Eastward Ho!*, and *The Revenger's Tragedy*.) Eld produced two issues of Q1. The second is distinguished by (i) an additional scene, IV, iv, printed on three leaves inserted between H3 and H4, with the instruction 'Place this at the latter end of the fourth Act' set in black-letter at the foot of the first page; and (ii) a cancel title-leaf (the fourth leaf of the sheet on which IV, iv was printed) advertising the fresh material. A second edition of the play followed in 1622. Its printer, Augustine Matthewes, was careful enough to work from a copy of the rarer second issue of Q1, but his edition is a straightforward line-for-line reprint, with no independent authority, often corrupt, and of little editorial value.

[48] 'Middleton's Tragicomedies', 16, 18.
[49] 'The First Edition of *A Faire Quarrell*', *Library* (Fifth Series), 4 (1949). 138.

The MS which underlies the first issue of Q1 was most probably a fair copy made by one or possibly both of the authors of their foul papers and intended for sale either to the acting company or to the publisher. The stage-direction is often careful and detailed (e.g., III, i, 111; III, ii, 15–22; V, i, 258), and on the whole much fuller than that of several Middleton plays most likely set from foul-paper copy.[50] It also takes on occasions the permissive or descriptive form which suggests authorial origin (e.g., I, i, 36; II, ii, 64; IV, i, 1). Though 'fair' rather than 'foul', the MS still retained various omissions and obscurities, and these argue against its having been edited or annotated in the playhouse. Several exits are missing, and mere numbers are occasionally used for speech-prefixes (with two pairs of unnamed 'friends' this is sometimes seriously confusing). Further, it is doubtful whether a prompter would have tolerated any of the following: (i) the failure to mark an entrance at V, i, 183; (ii) the inadequacy of the stage-direction at the beginning of IV, ii and its absence at V, i, 409–14; (iii) the vague and inconsistent designation of the Colonel's friends (the first friend is variously designated 'Col. 1. Friend', 'Colonels Second', '1 Liefetenant', and, apparently, merely 'Colonels Friend', while as the text stands the second friend is mute); (iv) the enigmatic '2 Roarer' in IV, i (no '1 Roarer' is mentioned). These stigmas, together with the general diversity in the spelling of speech-prefixes and the regular incidence of the authors' preferred contractional forms, indicate that the MS had not undergone the normalizing treatment it would have received from a professional scribe and was probably autograph.

Whether more likely in the autograph of one or of both of the authors it is impossible to determine. Commonsense suggests the former, especially since a printer or theatre book-holder would hardly have welcomed an assemblage of partially filled sheets written in different hands; yet the neat confinement of each author's distinctive linguistic pattern to different sections of the text goes against this.[51] If one of the authors did act as transcriber, the evidence,

---

[50] The quarto of *A Mad World*, for example, omits 13 entrances, that of *Your Five Gallants* 24, and that of *A Trick to Catch the Old One* (printed by Eld in 1608) 29.

[51] The only exception is IV, iii; see above, p. xxi. If one of the authors had made the fair copy, one would expect to find only the copyist's linguistic pattern in his own share of the play, and the share of his partner to contain a mixture of the preferred linguistic forms of both authors. This is the case with the text of Middleton and Dekker's *The Roaring Girl*, the quarto (1611) of which was printed from a fair copy prepared by Dekker; see G. R. Price, 'The MS and the Quarto of *The Roaring Girl*', *Library* (Fifth Series), 11 (1956), 181–2.

such as it is, favours Rowley: his share was much the larger, he contributed the preface (in which he ignores Middleton's co-authorship), and, more positively, Q1's style of act-division ('Actus primus, Scaena prima', etc.) is more like his than Middleton's.[52] Certainly Rowley must have been active in bringing such a new and popular play so promptly to the press. The policy of the acting companies, who 'usually . . . owned the copyright, as well as the stage-right, of plays', was to delay publication as long as a play was enjoying success in the theatre.[53] As leader of the troupe which owned *A Fair Quarrel*, Rowley was in a position to overrule customary procedure.

Two compositors set up the MS into type. One (= Compositor A) began the text on B1^r and continued to C4^v; the other (= B) then set gatherings D, E, and F; then A returned to complete the text with the probable exception of B's setting of a page in the last gathering, K1^r. Typographically, the two men's stints are readily distinguishable: A set from a different case and used a different fount of type for act-headings; he set more lines of type per page, used a wider measure for both verse and prose, and usually signed the fourth leaf of his gatherings. Further, of the four skeleton formes with which the text was imposed, two were employed in gatherings D, E, F and two in the remainder.

Only one of these features, the number of lines per page, suggests that K1^r was set by Compositor B; but firm support is provided by a variant spelling. A's (and probably Rowley's) spelling of 'Chough' was 'Chaugh' ('Chau.' in speech-prefixes): this is the spelling in gathering C and throughout G, H, I. In D, E, F it becomes 'Chawgh' or 'Chaw.', and there is a sudden return to this form at K1^r. That the discrepancy is compositorial, and not due to the authors or a scribe, is indicated by the authorship divisions for the play, which do not coincide with the incidence of the variant spellings, and by the fact that the transition from 'Chau.' on I4^v to 'Chaw.' on K1^r is accompanied by a change of sheet.

B seems to have been the more assertive and independent workman of the two. Though his gross blunders were proportionately fewer,

---

[52] This formula is used in Rowley's *A Match at Midnight*, and 'Actus Primus', 'Actus Secundus', etc. is used in *A New Wonder* and *All's Lost by Lust*. Middleton wrote 'Actus primi, Scaena prima', 'Finit Actus primus, Incipit Actus secundus', and so on; see Price, 'The Early Editions of *A Trick to Catch the Old One*', 207–8. Judging from the diverse styles of act-division in other plays printed by Eld, his compositors followed their copy in this respect (even if, as in *Troilus and Cressida*, the play was undivided).

[53] Evelyn M. Albright, *Dramatic Publication in England 1580–1640*, New York, 1927, p. 283. See also Chambers, III, 183ff.

he imposed a heavier style of punctuation, had an absolute preference for certain spellings (e.g., *here* rather than *heere*), strongly favoured others (e.g., a single rather than a double *e* ending in such words as *he*, *be*, etc.), and made some attempt to regularize the spelling of speech-prefixes.[54] Worse, one of his errors implies a readiness to sophisticate the sense of his copy: encountering the abbreviation 'M.' at II, ii, 1 he expanded it to 'Master', though the authors, intention was clearly 'Mistress'. (It is illuminating to compare I, i, 386 where A, finding the same abbreviation, set precisely what he saw before him.) Regarding A one should perhaps, as Housman remarked of medieval scribes, 'praise God for a simple fool'. His departures from copy—such as his mangling of the medical terms in IV, ii and V, i—were usually of the blatant, literal kind which are relatively easy to detect and emend.

Two other features of the composition of Q1 need to be noted. The pattern of recurring types and substituted sorts shows that setting was by formes, and it is clear that on several occasions miscalculations in casting-off obliged the compositor to expand or compress the text in order to fit it into the predetermined limits of the type-page. Extra white space was sometimes left around stage-directions, or single lines of verse were divided into two. When space needed to be saved, stage-directions were crowded in with the text, speeches set continuously, and verse set as prose. (At the foot of I4[v] (V, i, 338–42), for example, two lines were saved by this last method.) On only one occasion, however, at the foot of D2[r] (II, i, 177–8), is it likely that faulty casting-off provoked an actual omission.

The compositors were further harassed by having to use an unusually narrow measure for verse, presumably because neither of their cases was adequately supplied with quads. To squeeze in long lines they tinkered with spellings and removed spaces, abbreviated words with tildes and ampersands, omitted marks of punctuation (particularly at the ends of lines), folded final words over or under, and occasionally extended lines out beyond the measure, blocking them in later with 'quotations' (i.e., large units of spacing material).[55] More seriously, they sometimes resorted to mislineation, as in B1[v] (I, i, 50–1):

[54] Judging from the extant holograph MSS, both Middleton and Rowley punctuated lightly and preferred to write *hee*, *bee*, etc.
[55] This last expedient sometimes gives the right-hand margins a ragged appearance, making fold-overs and fold-unders look unnecessary and the catchword appear inset. It also led Price mistakenly to identify two compositors in D, E, and F ('The First Edition of *A Faire Quarrell*', 139).

> *Russ.* Heres noble youths, belike some wench has
> crost 'em,/and now they know not what to doe with
> their blood./

But again there is only one instance (II, i, 86) where this exigency
may have provoked serious interference, and one may be grateful
that the compositors did not solve their problems so simply and
drastically more often.

IV, iv, the scene added in the second issue of Q1, was probably
printed from a separate, theatrical MS. The spelling of speech-
prefixes is strikingly more uniform than elsewhere in Q1, suggesting
scribal transcription, and the stage-directions—'Hem, within' (l. 1),
'Iustle' (l. 53), 'Sing Baud' (l. 102)—take the elliptical, imperative
form usually associated with the prompter.[56] The bibliographical
evidence indicates that the MS did not arrive in Eld's shop until
well after the completion of the first issue. A single, new skeleton
was constructed with which to impose the additional material,
implying that the original Q1 skeletons had already been distributed,
and similarly the replacement title-page, though it did not differ
extensively from its predecessor, had to be entirely reset.[57] Further,
a comparison of watermarks shows that IV, iv was printed on a stock
of paper different from that which supplied the sheets for the first
issue, and the proportion of surviving first to second issue copies
—ten to three—indicates that most of the original Q1 copies had been
sold before the extra gathering was ready. It is likely, then, that
a lengthy interval—perhaps several months—occurred between
Trundle's acquisition of the first MS and his acquisition of the
second. The theory most consistent with the evidence is that he
obtained the second from the playhouse, having learnt of a stage-
revival of the play to which Rowley had contributed a new scene
(see also above, p. xiv).

All but one[58] of the thirteen extant Q1 copies have been collated
for the present edition. Some forty variants are apparent, about half
due to poor inking or loose type and the remainder to stop-press

[56] Although Greg, *The Shakespeare First Folio*, 1955, p. 124, impugns this
association as 'an old superstition', the sudden switch from the indicative
mood used elsewhere in Q1 seems significant.
[57] The same *F* was used in the main title of both title-pages, but this may be
put down to chance. Price, 'First Edition', 140–1, mistakenly claims that
(i) the first line is that of the original title-page; (ii) two skeletons were used
for the inserted gathering; (iii) they were those used for B-C, G-K. He takes
these 'facts' as evidence that 'the second issue followed closely on the first'.
[58] The first-issue copy in the Library of Congress, which is too fragile to be
photocopied.

correction, but of these last only three (I, i, 42; IV, i, 14, 167) significantly alter the text. All subsequent editions have also been collated, Dyce's, despite its cavalier handling of lineation and contractions, proving the most useful. In the present edition spelling and punctuation have been modernized, and phonetically redundant elisions silently expanded (thus, while *ath* remains as *o'th'*, *vnrauisht* becomes *unravished*). Q1's stage-directions and speech-prefixes have been regularized, additions to them enclosed in square brackets, and departures from Q1's text, in matters of substantives and lineation, noted at the foot of the page.

FURTHER READING

Bowers, F., 'Henry Howard Earl of Northampton and Duelling in England', *Englische Studien*, 71 (1936–37), 350–5.

Bowers, F., 'Middleton's *Fair Quarrel* and the Duelling Code', *JEGP*, 36 (1937), 40–65.

Bradbrook, M. C., *The Growth and Structure of Elizabethan Comedy*, 1955.

Bradbrook, M. C., *Themes and Conventions of Elizabethan Tragedy*, 1935.

Dunlap, R., 'James I, Bacon, Middleton, and the Making of *The Peacemaker*', *Studies in the English Renaissance Drama in Memory of K. J. Holzknecht*, ed. J. W. Bennett *et al.*, New York, 1959, pp. 82–94.

Ellis-Fermor, U. M., *The Jacobean Drama*, rev. edn., 1961.

Farr, Dorothy M., *Thomas Middleton and the Drama of Realism*, 1973.

Levin, R., *The Multiple Plot in English Renaissance Drama*, 1971.

Levin, R., 'Sexual Equations in the Elizabethan Double Plot', *Literature and Psychology*, 16 (1966), 2–14.

Peery, W., 'The Roaring Boy Again', *Shakespeare Association Bulletin*, 23 (1948), 12–16, 78–86.

Rabkin, N., 'The Double Plot: Notes on the History of a Convention', *Renaissance Drama*, 7 (1964), 55–69.

Robb, D. M., 'The Canon of William Rowley's Plays', *MLR*, 45 (1950) 129–41.

Schoenbaum, S., *Middleton's Tragedies: A Critical Study*, New York, 1955.

Schoenbaum, S., 'Middleton's Tragicomedies', *MP*, 54 (1956–57), 7–19.

Watson, C. B., *Shakespeare and the Renaissance Concept of Honour*, Princeton, 1960.

A Faire Quarrell.

With new Additions of M^r. *Chaughs* and
Trimtrams Roaring, and the Bauds Song.
Neuer before Printed.

As it was Acted before the King, by the Prince
his Highnesse Seruants.

{ Written by *Thomas Midleton*, }
{ and *William Rowley*. } Gent.

Printed at London for *I. T.* and are to be sold at Chrift
Church Gate. 1617.

A Faire Quarrell. The title is designed to raise the topical question of the ethics of duelling: it echoes a stock formula current among duellists which was frequently attacked by judges and anti-duelling pamphleteers. Edward Sackville, for example, used it in 1613 in his reply to a challenge from Lord Bruce of Kinloss: 'As it shalbe allwaies far from me to seeke a quarrell, soe will I allwaies be readie to meete any that desire to make triall of my valor by soe faire a course as you requier' (quoted by G. P. V. Akrigg, *Jacobean Pageant*, 1962, p. 254); and the following year James I, alarmed by the steady depletion of his courtiers, decreed that in future the law would 'proceede capitallie against all those that are found to speede their enemies vpon priuate Quarrells in the Fields after a faire maner, (according to the phrase) that is, without treacherie or fraud' (*His Majesty's Edict and Severe Censure against Private Combats and Combatants*, 1614, p. 6). 'Fair' is also a key word in the play itself, occurring in a wide variety of senses (e.g., 'beautiful', 'specious', 'morally just', 'noble', 'genuine', 'according to the rules') as the play works out its definition of honour. For an informative, though critically misguided, discussion of this aspect of the play, see Fredson Bowers, 'Middleton's *Fair Quarrel* and the Duelling Code', *JEGP*, 36 (1937), 40–65. Finally, it is worth noting, since this is often overlooked, that 'A Fair Quarrel'—like the title of *The Changeling*—is a title which can be applied with equal appropriateness to each of the play's separate plots.

new Additions. The tautological phrase was regularly used of interpolated material; cf. V, i, 420, and Middleton's *The Mayor of Queenborough*, V, i, 231–2: 'A pox on your new additions! they spoil all the plays that ever they come in'.

Woodcut. Probably copied out of one of the many fencing manuals, whose instructional diagrams are often similar though less detailed (note the discarded hats and scabbards). An illustration of the much-favoured 'low ward' is apparently intended, but A. L. Soens warns that the accuracy of all such contemporary diagrams 'must be viewed with grave suspicion' ('Two Rapier Points: Analysing Elizabethan Fighting Methods', *NQ*, 213 (1968), 127). Care has been taken to distinguish the duellists, the means being probably suggested by I, i, 84.

To the nobly disposed, virtuous, and faithful-
breasted ROBERT GREY Esquire, one of the
grooms of his Highness' bed-chamber,
his poor well-willer wisheth
his best wishes, *hic et*   5
supra.

Worthy Sir,

'Tis but a play, and a play is but a butt, against which
many shoot many arrows of envy; 'tis the weaker part, and
how much more noble shall it be in you to defend it. Yet if it   10
be (as some philosophers have left behind 'em) that this
megacosm, this great world, is no more than a stage, where
every one must act his part, you shall of necessity have many
part-takers, some long, some short, some indifferent, all some;
whilst indeed the players themselves have the least part of it,   15
for I know few that have lands (which are a part of the world),
and therefore no grounded men; but howsoever they serve
for mutes, happily they must wear good clothes for attendance.

---

  3 *his Highness* Prince Charles
  8 *butt* target in archery. Cf. I, i, 120
12 *megacosm* macrocosm. *OED*'s earliest example
14 *indifferent* medium, average
    all some i.e., all playing some part
17 *no grounded men* (i) of no fixed abode (ii) lacking education
    howsoever to whatever extent
18 *mutes* actors without speaking parts

---

  2 ROBERT GREY. 'Perhaps Rowley as leader of the Prince's company had
dealings with Grey about court performances before the company's
patron' (Bentley, II, 1018). Nothing is known about Grey, though he
may be the 'Robert Graye' who received an M.A. at Cambridge in 1612
on the visit of Prince Charles (see J. and J. A. Venn, *Alumni
Cantabrigienses*, Part I, 4 vols., 1922–27, II, 252). The coincidence of
names is suggestive.
10–13 *Yet . . . part.* Jaques's famous lines in *As You Like It*, II, vii, 139–41
might suggest Shakespeare as the 'philosopher' Rowley has in mind,
but the world-stage metaphor was a commonplace (see Anne Righter,
Shakespeare and the Idea of the Play, 1962, pp. 64, 165).
14 *part-takers* Q1 (partakers Q2). Q1's division of the word between two
lines caused the Q2 compositor and all later editors to overlook the
characteristic Rowley quibble.

Yet all have exits, and must all be stripped in the tiring-house
(viz. the grave), for none must carry anything out of the stock.   20
You see, sir, I write as I speak, and I speak as I am, and that's
excuse enough for me. I did not mean to write an epistle of
praise to you; it looks so like a thing I know you love not,
flattery, which you exceedingly hate actively, and unpleasingly
accept passively: indeed, I meant to tell you your own, that is,   25
that this child of the Muses is yours; whoever begat it, 'tis
laid to your charge, and (for aught I know) you must father and
keep it too. If it please you, I hope you shall not be ashamed
of it neither, for it has been seen (though I say it) in good
companies, and many have said it is a handsome pretty-spoken   30
infant. Now be your own judge: at your leisure look on it, at
your pleasure laugh at it; and if you be sorry it is no better,
you may be glad it is no bigger.

Yours ever,

William Rowley.   35

---

19 *tiring-house* dressing-room

20 *none . . . stock.* A provision in Philip Henslowe's contract with the actor
   Robert Dawes signed in 1614 (see W. W. Greg, ed., *Henslowe Papers*,
   1907, pp. 123–5). The fine for infringement was 40 pounds.

26 *child of the Muses.* A literary cliché which Rowley similarly elaborates
   in his Address to the Reader prefixed to *The World Tossed at Tennis*
   (Bullen, VII, 143–4). Cf. the dedication to Robert Keysar in *The Knight
   of the Burning Pestle.*

29–30 *good companies.* Probably an allusion to the performance 'before the
   King' mentioned on the title-page of Q1.

[DRAMATIS PERSONAE

RUSSELL, *father to Jane and brother to Lady Ager*
CAPTAIN AGER, *son to Lady Ager*
THE COLONEL
FITZALLEN, *his kinsman, secretly married to Jane*
CHOUGH, *a foolish gentleman of Cornwall*   5
TRIMTRAM, *his man*
TWO FRIENDS *to Captain Ager*
TWO FRIENDS *to the Colonel*
PHYSICIAN
SURGEON   10
USHER *of the Roaring-School*
CAPTAIN ALBO, *an Irish pander*
VAPOUR, *a tobacco-man*
Sergeants, Roarers, Servants

LADY AGER   15
JANE
THE COLONEL'S SISTER
ANNE, *sister to the Physician*

2 AGER. W. Power suggests that Ager's name puns on *eager* (the first syllable of which was 'pronounced by Jacobeans to rhyme with *may*'), thus 'pointing to his eager spirit' ('Middleton's Way with Names', *NQ*, 205 (1960), 140). Perhaps so, but a play on '(duelling–) field' (Latin *ager*) is also intended.

5 CHOUGH. A type-name which implies its bearer's place of origin as well as his character. The Cornish chough (now called the red-legged crow) was a sea-bird: 'his bil is sharpe, long and red, his legs of the same colour' (R. Carew, *The Survey of Cornwall*, 1602, f. 36ʳ). 'Chough' also meant 'rustic, clown, boor' (*OED, s.v.* 'chuff'), particularly of the rich and gullible variety, and Dyce, quoting R. Brathwaite's *The Honest Ghost*, 1658, p. 167, notes that 'Cornish chough' itself seems to have been used in this sense: 'a Country gull,/Whose fathers death had made his pockets full,/ . . . this *Cornish-Chough* mourns for his father/In a *Carnation feather*'. The name also carried an implication of obesity (see *1 Henry IV*, II, ii, 86; Nashe, I, 163). If Rowley himself first acted Chough, the connotation would not have lacked point (see above, p. xii).

16 JANE. Power (p. 58) thinks the name appropriate to 'a likeable but not particularly complex heroine'. Middleton in *No Wit, No Help* and Rowley in *A New Wonder, a Woman Never Vexed* had already given the name to very similar characters.

DUTCH NURSE
MEG, *a bawd*   20
PRISS, *a whore*

The Scene: London]

21 PRISS. Intended, as Power notes (op. cit., 140), as a gibe at the Puritans, since *Priscilla* was 'one of the great Puritan names'.

A FAIR QUARREL

Act I, Scene i

Enter Master RUSSELL, *solus*

RUSSELL

It must be all my care; there's all my love,
And that pulls on the tother. Had I been left
In a son behind me, while I had been here
He should have shifted as I did before him,
Lived on the freeborn portion of his wit;   5
But a daughter, and that an only one—Oh!
We cannot be too careful o'her, too tender;
'Tis such a brittle niceness, a mere cupboard of glasses,
The least shake breaks or cracks 'em. All my aim is
To cast her upon riches: that's the thing   10
We rich men call perfection, for the world
Can perfect nought without it. 'Tis not neatness,
Either in handsome wit or handsome outside,
With which one gentleman—far in debt—has courted her,
Which boldness he shall rue. He thinks me blind   15
And ignorant: I have let him play a long time,
Seemed to believe his worth, which I know nothing;
He may perhaps laugh at my easy confidence
Which closely I requite upon his fondness,
For this hour snaps him; and before his mistress,   20
His 'saint', forsooth, which he inscribes my girl,

---

2 *tother* common form or 'other'
4 *shifted* managed   8 *niceness* delicacy
12 *neatness* refinement, good breeding
19 *fondness* (i) folly (ii) affectionateness
20 *snaps him* catches him unawares

---

7 *o'her* ed. (ore Q1). This has a better claim than 'or', which nowhere
appears in Q1 with a final *e*. Cf. Middleton's contractional form *has* ('he
has').
8–9 *'Tis . . . 'em.* Proverbial; cf. Tilley, G134, W646, one of whose
examples illuminates the mercenary motives behind Russell's fatherly
concern: 'women having lost their chastity are like broken glasses
which are good for nothing'.
17 *worth.* Russell means 'wealth' not 'worthiness'. Cf. his use at l.36.
21 *inscribes.* Russell has been reading Jane's letters.

7

He shall be rudely taken and disgraced.
The trick will prove an everlasting scarecrow
To fright poor gallants from our rich men's daughters.

Enter the LADY AGER, *with two* SERVANTS

Sister! I've such a joy to make you a welcome of,   25
Better you never tasted.
LADY AGER
                    Good sir, spare it not.
RUSSELL
Colonel's come, and your son, Captain Ager.
LADY AGER.
My son!   *She weeps*
RUSSELL
          I know your eye would be first served;
That's the soul's taster still for grief or joy.
LADY AGER
Oh, if a mother's dear suit may prevail with him,   30
From England he shall never part again.
RUSSELL
No question he'll be ruled, and grant you that.
LADY AGER
I'll bring all my desires to that request.
                    Exeunt LADY *and her* SERVANTS
RUSSELL
Affectionate sister, she has no daughter now;
It follows all the love must come to him,   35
And he has a worth deserves it, were it dearer.

          Enter a FRIEND *of the* COLONEL'*s, and another*
                    of CAPTAIN AGER'*s*

COLONEL'S FRIEND
I must not give way to't.
RUSSELL [*Aside*]
                    What's here to question?

---

29 *taster* servant who tastes his master's food to ascertain its
     quality or to detect poison (*for* = 'for the detection of')
     still always

---

27 *Colonel.* Pronounced then as spelled (Sampson).
28 s.d. Middleton's characters often express joy by weeping; cf. *The
     Phoenix*, V, i, 56; *The Old Law*, IV, ii, 35; *The Changeling*, III, iv, 24
30–1 See II, i, 35–40 and note.

COLONEL'S FRIEND

  Compare young Captain Ager with the Colonel!

CAPTAIN'S FRIEND

  Young? why, do you make youth stand for an imputation?
  That which you now produce for his disgrace   40
  Infers his nobleness, that being young
  Should have an anger more inclined to wisdom
  And moderation than the Colonel:
  A virtue as rare as chastity in youth;
  And let the cause be good—conscience in him,   45
  Which ever crowns his acts, and is indeed
  Valour's prosperity—he dares then as much
  As ever made him famous that you plead for.

COLONEL'S FRIEND

  Then I forbear too long.

CAPTAIN'S FRIEND

                  His worth for me!

                      [*They draw and fight*]

RUSSELL

  Here's noble youths; belike some wench has crossed 'em,   50
  And now they know not what to do with their blood.

39–40 prose in Q1   45 *conscience* i.e., this is a matter of conscience
50 *crossed* disappointed, jilted   50–1 prose in Q1
51 *blood* punning on *blood* = 'sexual desire'

---

42 *wisdom.* The reading of only one of the extant copies of Q1. The other
twelve read *courage*, and are followed by Q2 and all previous editors
(though probably because they were unaware of a press-variant). It
cannot be established bibliographically which state is the earlier, since
this is the only correction in the forme and it was made without
disturbance to type. *Wisdom*, however, gives much the better reading.
Conscientiousness not courage is at issue, and wisdom rather than
courage was proverbially 'rare . . . in youth'. Cf. I, i, 126 and IV, iii, 40;
and note especially V. Saviolo, *Vincentio Saviolo his Practice*, 1595, sig.
Bb1ʳ: 'the wisdom and discretion of a man, is as great a vertue as his
magnanimitie and courage, which are so much the greater vertues, by
how much they are accompanied with wisedome: for without them a
man is not to be accounted valiant but rather furious'.

44 A startling simile, linking the military and sexual themes of the play.
Chastity is an obsessive concern in Middleton; cf. *More Dissemblers*, I,
ii, 84–5: 'the chasteness of his continence . . . a rare grace in the spring
of man'.

49 s.d. Such an eruption may seem improbable, but soldiers were noted to
be 'Jealous in honour, sudden and quick in quarrel' (*As You Like It*,
II, vii, 151); 'he argues sharply, and carries his conclusion in his
scabberd' (T. Overbury, 'A Souldier', *Characters*, 1614).

Enter the COLONEL *and* CAPTAIN AGER

COLONEL
How now!
CAPTAIN AGER
   Hold, hold, what's the incitement?
COLONEL
So serious at your game? Come, come, the quarrel.
COLONEL'S FRIEND
Nothing, good faith, sir.
COLONEL
     Nothing, and you bleed?
COLONEL'S FRIEND
Bleed? where? pish, a little scratch by chance, sir. 55
COLONEL
What need this niceness, when you know so well
That I must know these things, and truly know 'em?
Your daintiness makes me but more impatient;
This strange concealment frets me.
COLONEL'S FRIEND
      Words did pass
Which I was bound to answer as my opinion 60
And love instructed me;
And should I take in general fame into 'em,
I think I should commit no error in't.
COLONEL
What words, sir, and of whom?
COLONEL'S FRIEND
      This gentleman
Paralleled Captain Ager's worth with yours. 65
COLONEL
With mine?
COLONEL'S FRIEND
   It was a thing I could not listen to
With any patience.
CAPTAIN AGER
    What should ail you, sir?
There was little wrong done to your friend i'that.

61–3 *lineation* ed.
62 *take in ... into 'em* include ... with them. *OED* cites no such
  usage before 1647 ('take', *v.*, 82.k)
  fame reputation
66 *not* ed. (nor Q1)

COLONEL

How! little wrong to me?

CAPTAIN AGER

                              I said so, friend,

And I suppose that you'll esteem it so.   70

COLONEL

Comparisons!

CAPTAIN AGER

                    Why, sir, 'twixt friend and friend

There is so even and level a degree

It will admit of no superlative.

COLONEL

Not in terms of manhood?

RUSSELL

                              Nay, gentlemen—

COLONEL

Good sir, give me leave.—In terms of manhood   75

What can you dispute more questionable?

You are a captain, sir; I give you all your due.

CAPTAIN AGER

And you are a colonel, a title

Which may include within it many captains;

Yet, sir, but throwing by those titular shadows,   80

Which add no substance to the men themselves,

And take them uncompounded, man and man,

They may be so with fair equality.

COLONEL

Y'are a boy, sir.

---

71 *Comparisons* cf. the proverb 'Comparisons are odious' (Tilley, C576)

---

77 *captain.* Commanded a company of about 200 foot. The rank was 'not lightlie to be considered of, for that vppon his skill and knowledge dependeth the safety or losse of many men's liues' (G. Clayton, *The Approved Order of Martial Discipline*, 1591, p. 11). As the corruptibility of captains in the English army in the Netherlands had been a common scandal, a Jacobean audience would have been particularly impressed by Ager's ideals.

78 *colonel.* Commander of a regiment and subordinate only to the general and his staff; 'so farre transcending all others which are of any rank below him, that as *Pharohs* Tower, he should be a Lanthorne to guide euery wandering Souldier to the perfection of his duty' (F. Markham, *Five Decades of Epistles of War*, 1622, p. 162). Not instituted until the end of the 16th century, this is the first appearance of the rank on the English stage.

CAPTAIN AGER
                    And you have a beard, sir;
Virginity and marriage are both worthy,   85
And the positive purity there are some
Have made the nobler.
COLONEL
                              How now?
RUSSELL
                                        Nay, good sir—
CAPTAIN AGER
    I shrink not: he that goes the foremost
May be o'ertaken.
COLONEL
                    Death, how am I weighed?
CAPTAIN AGER
    In an even balance, sir; a beard put in   90
Gives but a small advantage: man and man,
And lift the scales.
COLONEL
                    Patience shall be my curse
    If it ride me further!   [*They draw their swords*]
RUSSELL
                    How now, gallants?
Believe me, then, I must give aim no longer.
Can words beget swords and bring 'em forth, ha?   95
Come, they are abortive propagations;
Hide 'em, for shame. I had thought soldiers
Had been musical, would not strike out of time,
But to the consort of drum, trumps, and fife:
'Tis madman-like to dance without music,   100

89 *weighed* esteemed. Ager plays on the literal sense to make way
   for his taunting rejoinder
93 *ride* rule
98 *strike out of time* (i) fail to keep time (ii) fight at an inappropriate
   time
99 *consort* harmonious accompaniment

90–1 *a . . . advantage.* Cf. 'Wisdom consists not in a beard' and 'An old
   goat is never the more reverend for his beard' (Tilley, W524, G199).
   To be refuted by a glib appeal to a proverbial platitude is of course all
   the more galling.
94 *give aim.* Stand idly by. Weakened metaphoric sense from the original
   meaning, in archery, 'to guide one in his aim by informing him of the
   result of a preceding shot' (*OED*, 'aim', *sb.*, 3.b).

And most unpleasing shows to the beholders;
A Lydian ditty to a Doric note.
Friends embrace with steel hands? fie, it meets too hard:
I must have those encounters here debarred.

COLONEL
Shall I lose here what I have safe brought home   105
Through many dangers?

CAPTAIN AGER
                              What's that, sir?

COLONEL
                                             My fame,
Life of the life, my reputation:
Death! I am squared and measured out; my heights,
Depths, breadth, all my dimensions taken!
Sure I have yet beyond your astralobe   110
A spirit unbounded.

CAPTAIN AGER
                         Sir, you might weigh—

RUSSELL
Tush! all this is weighing fire, vain and fruitless;
The further it runs into argument,
The further plunged: beseech you, no more on't.
I have a little claim, sir, in your blood,   115
As near as the brother to your mother;
If that may serve for power to move your quiet,
The rest I shall make up with courtesy
And an uncle's love.

CAPTAIN AGER
                         I have done, sir, but—

RUSSELL
But! I'll have no more shooting at these butts.   120

102 *A . . . note* a gentle song to a rude air (Sampson)
103 *it . . . hard* (i) that is too inappropriate (ii) it (the embrace) is too
     rough
106 *fame* reputation. Cf. II, i, 44, 69, 102
108 *squared* marked off in squares
110 *astralobe* common 17th-century spelling of 'astrolabe', an instru-
     ment used to take altitudes
120 *butts* see dedicatory epistle, l.8

112 *weighing fire.* 'Then he said unto me, Goe thy way, weigh me the
     weight of the fire, or measure me the blast of the wind, or call me again
     the day that is past' (*Apocrypha*, 2 Esdras iv. 5).

COLONEL

We'll to pricks when he please.

RUSSELL

                                        You rove all still.

Sir, I have no motive proof to disgest

Your raised choler back into temperate blood;

But if you'll make mine age a counsellor,

As all ages have hitherto allowed it—   125

Wisdom in men grows up as years increase—

You shall make me blessed in making peace,

And do your judgement right.

COLONEL

                                        In peace at home

Grey hairs are senators, but to determine

Soldiers and their actions—

Enter FITZALLEN *and* JANE

RUSSELL

                                        'Tis peace here, sir;   130

And see, here comes a happy interim:

Here enters now a scene of loving arms;

This couple will not quarrel so.

COLONEL'S FRIEND [*Aside to* COLONEL]

                                        Be advised, sir;

This gentleman, Fitzallen, is your kinsman:

You may o'erthrow his long-laboured fortunes   135

With one angry minute; 'tis a rich churl,

And this his sole inheritrix: blast not

His hopes with this tempest.

COLONEL

                                        It shall calm me;

121 *pricks* pun involving *prick* = (i) bull's-eye (ii) sword
   You . . . still probably 'you are still not following the correct
   course'. To *rove* an arrow was to shoot it away from the mark
   (*OED*, *v.*, 2)
122 *disgest* digest
127 *You . . . peace* 'Blessed are the peacemakers' (Matthew v. 9)
131 *interim* interlude

122–3 *no . . . blood.* No argument compelling enough to assuage your anger
   and thus restore your blood to its correct 'temperature' (in which the
   four humours are equally balanced).

All the town's conjurors and their demons
Could not have laid my spirit so.
FITZALLEN

                       Worthy coz,   140
I gratulate your fair return to peace;
Your swift fame was at home long before you.
COLONEL
It meets, I hope, your happy fortunes here,
And I am glad in't. I must salute your joys, coz,
With a soldier's encounter.   *Kisses her*
FITZALLEN

               Worthy Captain Ager;   145
I hope my kinsman shortly.
RUSSELL [*Aside*]

              You must come short indeed,
Or the length of my device will be ill-shrunk.—
Why, now it shows finely! I'll tell you, sir—
Sir? nay, son: I know i'th' end 'twill be so—
FITZALLEN
I hope so, sir.
RUSSELL

         Hope? nay, 'tis past all hope, son.   150
Here has been such a stormy encounter
Betwixt my cousin captain and this brave colonel,
About I know not what—nothing indeed—
Competitions, degrees, and comparatives
Of soldiership; but this smooth passage   155
Of love has calmed it all. Come, I'll have't sound;
Let me see your hearts combined in your hands,

141 *gratulate* welcome
146 *come short* fall short, fail
150 *past all hope* (i) confirmed (ii) hopeless. Russell is playing with his
    victim
152 *cousin* used familiarly to express various degrees of relationship
    (Ellis)
155 *passage* (i) voyage (ii) interchange

---

139 *conjurors*. Wizards. The depreciated modern sense of 'entertainers
    who perform magical tricks' is not found before the 18th century.
140 *laid my spirit*. (i) prevented my ghost from walking (ii) calmed my
    feelings (of anger). Cf. Middleton's *The Puritan*, III, ii, 101 : 'The name
    of Coniurer has laid my blood'.
147 Or it is my stratagem that is ill-prepared and will 'come short'. An
    'ill-shrunk' garment would shrink again when washed; cf. *1 Henry IV*,
    V, iv, 88.

And then I will believe the league is good:
It shall be the grape's if we drink any blood.
COLONEL
  I have no anger, sir.
CAPTAIN AGER
                       I have had none,   160
My blood has not yet rose to a quarrel;
Nor have you had cause—
COLONEL
                        No cause of quarrel?
Death! if my father should tell me so—
RUSSELL
                     Again?

FITZALLEN
  Good sir, for my sake—
COLONEL
                Faith, I have done, coz;
You do too hastily believe mine anger;   165
And yet, to say diminiting valour
In a soldier is no cause of quarrel—
RUSSELL
Nay then, I'll remove the cause to kill th'effect.
Kinsman, I'll press you to't—if either love
Or consanguinity may move you to't—   170
I must disarm you: though ye're a soldier,
Pray grant me your weapon; it shall be safe
At your regress from my house. Now I know
                       [*Gives him his sword*]
No words can move this noble soldier's sword
To a man undefenced so. We shall parle,   175
And safely make all perfect friends again.

---

175 *parle* parley

163 *father*. Bowers notes that the remark is 'calculated to prove . . . to
    what dizzy heights the Colonel would uphold his sense of honour', and
    quotes L. Briskett, *A Discourse of Civil Life*, 1606, p. 74: '[duellists] are
    not ashamed to say . . . that a man for cause of honor may arme
    himself . . . euen against his father, and with cursed hands violate his
    person' ('Duelling Code', 45).
166 *diminiting*. Not in *OED*. One is tempted to emend to 'diminishing', but
    Rowley was fond of this type of Latin coinage.
168 *I'll . . . effect*. A loose version of the scholastic tag, *ablata causa, tollitur
    effectus*, similarly adapted in *The Changeling*, II, vi, 52.

COLONEL

   To show my will, sir, accept mine to you:
   As good not wear it as not dare to use it.

COLONEL'S FRIEND

   Nay then, sir, we will be all exampled:
   We'll have no arms here now but lovers' arms.   180

CAPTAIN'S FRIEND

   No seconds must begin a quarrel: take mine sir.

RUSSELL

   Why, law, what a fine sunshine's here! These clouds
   My breath has blown into another climate.
   I'll be your armourers: they are not pawned.
   [*Aside*] These were the fish that I did angle for;   185
   I have caught 'em finely; now for my trick:
   My project's lusty, and will hit the nick.   *Exit with weapons*

COLONEL

   What, is't a match, beauty? I would now have
   Alliance with my worthy Captain Ager,
   To knit our loves the faster: here's witness   190
   Enough if you confirm it now.

JANE

                     Sir, my voice
   Was long since given, since that I gave my hand.

COLONEL

   Would you had sealed too!

JANE

               That wish comes too late,
   For I too soon fear my delivery.—   *Aside*
   My father's hand sticks yet, sir; you may now   195
   Challenge a lawful interest in his:

181 lineation ed. (Take . . . sir Q1 as separate line)
182 *law* exclamation, meaningless in itself, marking an emphatic statement
182–3 prose in Q1   187 *nick* exact point aimed at

---

182 *sunshine's*. Q1's 'Sun shines' is ambiguous, but cf. I, i, 394 (here Q1 reads 'sun-shine').
188–93 The Colonel suggests a *de praesenti* betrothal, but Jane reveals that this has already occurred: she has given her 'voice' (the necessary *per verba* agreement) and her 'hand' (*handfasting* meant 'betrothal'). The Colonel's reply refers to the sanctifying of the match *in facie ecclesiae*, which has not yet taken place (see II, ii, 85–8).
194 *delivery*. (i) formal transfer of a document (ii) giving birth to a child. Rowley uses the same pun in *A New Wonder*, I, i, pp. 99–100.

He took your hand from your enraged blood,
And gave it freely to your opposite,
My cousin Ager; methinks you should claim from him,
In the less quality of calmer blood,   200
To join the hands of two divided friends,
Even these two that would offer willingly
Their own embrace.

CAPTAIN'S FRIEND
                    Troth, she instructs you well,
Colonel, and you shall do a lover's part
Worth one brave act of valour.

COLONEL
                            Why, I did   205
Misdoubt no scruple; is there doubt in it?

FITZALLEN
Faith, sir, delays, which at the least are doubts;
But here's a constant resolution fixed,
Which we wish willingly he would accord to.

COLONEL
Tush, he shall do't, I will not be denied;   210
He owes me so much in the recompense
Of my reconcilement.—Captain Ager,
You will take our parts against your uncle
In this quarrel?

CAPTAIN AGER
                I shall do my best, sir;
Two denials shall not repulse me; I love   215
Your worthy kinsman, and wish him mine; I know
He doubts it not.

COLONEL
            See, he's returned.

Enter RUSSELL *and a* SERVANT

RUSSELL [*Aside to* SERVANT]
                        Your cue,
Be sure you keep it; 'twill be spoken quickly,
Therefore watch it.   [*Exit* SERVANT]

198 *opposite* adversary
200 *less* lesser
206 *Misdoubt no scruple* have no doubts whatsoever

203–5 *Troth . . . valour.* All editors except Sampson re-assign this speech to
    the Colonel's friend without explanation or authority.

COLONEL
                    Let's set on him all at once.
OMNES
    Sir, we have a suit to you.
RUSSELL
                        What, all at once?   220
OMNES
    All, all, i'faith, sir.
RUSSELL
    One speaker may yet deliver: say, say;
    I shall not dare to stand out against so many.
COLONEL
    Faith, sir, here's a brabbling matter hangs on demur;
    I make the motion for all without a fee;   225
    Pray you, let it be ended this term.
RUSSELL
    Ha, ha, ha!
    That's the rascal's cue, and he has missed it.   *Aside*
    What is it, what is it, sir?
COLONEL
                        Why, sir, here's a man
    And here's a woman: y'are scholar good enough;   230
    Put 'em together and tell me what it spells.
RUSSELL
    Ha, ha, ha!
    There's his cue once again—

                    Enter SERVANT

                    Oh, he's come—hum.

SERVANT
    [*Aside*] My master laughs; that's his cue to mischief.
COLONEL
    What say you, sir?
SERVANT
                Sir—

224 *brabbling* cavilling, contentious
    demur objection. A legal term; cf. *OED*, 'demurrer', *sb.*¹, 1
226 *term* see note to V. i, 239
232–3 lineation ed. (Ha . . . agen,/Oh . . . humh Q1)

225 *motion.* 'An application made to a court or judge by a party to an
    action or his counsel to obtain some rule or Order of Court necessary to
    the progress of the action [here, Jane's marriage]' (*OED*, *sb.*, 8.b).

RUSSELL

Ha! what say you, sir?   235

SERVANT

Sir, there's a couple desire speedily to speak with you.

RUSSELL

A couple, sir, of what? hounds? or horses?

SERVANT

Men, sir; gentlemen or yeomen, I know not which,
But the one, sure, they are.

RUSSELL

Hast thou no other description of them?   240

SERVANT

They come with commission, they say, sir, to taste of your
earth; if they like it, they'll turn it into gunpowder.

RUSSELL

Oh, they are saltpetre-men; before me,
And they bring commission, the King's power indeed!
They must have entrance; but the knaves will be bribed: 245
There's all the hope we have in officers;
They were too dangerous in a commonwealth,
But that they will be very well corrupted;
Necessary varlets!

SERVANT

Shall I enter in, sir?

RUSSELL

By all fair means, sir,   250
And with all speed, sir; give 'em very good words
To save my ground unravished, unbroke up.

                              [*Exit* SERVANT]

---

243 *before me* an asseveration
248–9 *But . . . varlets* one line in Q1
250 *enter in* show them in

---

243 *saltpetre-men.* At this time saltpetre was obtained from earth impreg-
    nated with dung and, as the chief constituent of gunpowder, was
    claimed by the Crown. Saltpetre-men were empowered to enter any
    premises to search for suitable material. Their commission was widely
    resented; cf. Nashe, *an Almond for a Parrot*, 1590 (Nashe, III, 355):
    'saltpetermen . . . vndoing of poore men by dyggyng up their floars and
    breaking down their wals'.
245–9 *but . . . varlets.* A sly piece of irony: Russell has already proved the
    truth of his statement by bribing the officers to arrest Fitzallen on a
    trumped-up charge. Note that *varlet* meant 'sergeant' as well as
    'knave'.

Mine's yet a virgin earth; the worm hath not been seen
To wriggle in her chaste bowels; and I'd be loth
A gunpowder fellow should deflower her now.   255
COLONEL
Our suit is yet delayed by this means, sir.
RUSSELL
Alas, I cannot help it; these fellows gone,
As I hope I shall despatch 'em quickly,
A few articles shall conclude your suit.
Who, Master Fitzallen?—The only man   260
That my adoption aims at.
COLONEL
                    There's good hope then.

Enter two SERGEANTS *in disguise*

1 SERGEANT
Save you, sir.
RUSSELL
You are welcome, sir, for aught I know yet.
2 SERGEANT
We come to take a view and taste of your ground, sir.
RUSSELL
I had rather feed you with better meat,   265
Gentlemen, but do your pleasures, pray.
1 SERGEANT
This is our pleasures: we arrest you, sir,
In the King's name.

---

259 *articles* conditions in a legal agreement (taking up the Colonel's
    metaphor at ll.224–6)
261 *adoption* more sardonic word-play: (i) taking as a relation (ii)
    stratagem
265 *meat* food (i.e., Fitzallen)
265–6 lineation ed.   267–8 *This . . . name* one line in Q1

253–5 *Mine's . . . now.* A veiled comment on Fitzallen's wooing of Jane;
    doubly ironical since, unknown to Russell, the defloration has already
    occurred.
253 *worm.* Carrying a phallic reference, as in Marvell's 'To His Coy
    Mistress', ll.27–30.
261 s.d. *in disguise.* The ruse testifies to Russell's cunning, but it also
    illustrates the sergeant's traditional venality and his notoriously under-
    hand methods of attaching his victim: 'He goes muffled like a theefe
    and carryes still the markes of one, for he steales vpon a man cowardly'
    (Overbury, *Characters*, 'A Sarieant').

FITZALLEN
                    Ha! at whose suit?
RUSSELL
                              How's that?
COLONEL
    Our weapons, good sir; furnish us!
JANE
                              Ay me!
RUSSELL
    Stay, stay, gentlemen; let's enquire the cause;   270
    It may be but a trifle: a small debt
    Shall need no rescue here.
2 SERGEANT
    Sir, betwixt three creditors, Master Leech, Master Swallow,
    and Master Bonesuck, the debts are a thousand pounds.
RUSSELL
    A thousand pounds? beshrew me, a good man's substance!   275
COLONEL
    Good sir, our weapons! we'll teach these varlets
    To walk in their own parti-coloured coats,
    That they may be distinguished from honest men.
1 SERGEANT
    Sir, attempt no rescue; he's our prisoner:
    You'll make the danger worse by violence.   280
COLONEL
    A plague upon your gunpowder-treason!
    Ye quick-damned varlets,
    Is this your saltpetre-proving, your tasting earth?
    Would you might never feed better, nor none

272 *rescue* in the special sense of 'removal by force from legal
    custody'. Cf. *The Comedy of Errors*, IV, iv, 107–8
275 lineation ed. (Beshrow . . . substance Q1 as separate line)
276–80 prose in Q1
277 *parti-coloured coats* worn by minor civil officers
281 *gunpowder-treason* an early name for the Gunpowder Plot of 1605
282 *quick-damned* either 'damned quickly' or 'damned while still alive'.
    Probably a play on both is intended
282–6 *Ye . . . him* lineation ed.   283 *proving* testing

273–4 *Leech . . . Swallow . . . Bonesuck*. Self-explanatory names for usurers.
    Middleton had used this kind of nomenclature frequently in his city
    comedies.
275 *good . . . substance*. Like Shylock, Russell equates virtue with wealth; cf.
    The Merchant of Venice, I, iii, 12–17.

Of your catchpoll tribe!—Our weapons, good sir,   285
We'll yet deliver him.

RUSSELL

              Pardon me, sir,
I dare not suffer rescue here, at least
Not be so great an accessary
As to furnish you; had you had your weapons—
But to see the ill fate on't! [*Aside*] My fine trick, i'faith: 290
Let beggars beware to love rich men's daughters;
I'll teach 'em the new morris; I learnt it
Myself of another careful father.

FITZALLEN

May I not be bailed?

2 SERGEANT

            Yes, but not with swords.

COLONEL

Slaves, here are sufficient men!

1 SERGEANT

                   Ay, i'th' field,   295
But not in the city. Sir, if this gentleman
Will be one, we'll easily admit the second.

RUSSELL

Who, I? Sir, pray pardon me; I am wronged,
Very much wronged in this; I must needs speak it.—
Sir, you have not dealt like an honest lover,   300
With me nor my child: here you boast to me
Of a great revenue, a large substance,
Wherein you would endow and state my daughter;
Had I missed this, my opinion yet
Thought you a frugal man, to understand   305
The sure wards against all necessities;

285 *catchpoll* contemptuous name for a sergeant, especially in his capacity of arresting for debt
295 *sufficient* capable
297 *one* i.e., one of the two persons required to stand surety for bail
303 *state* instate. *OED*'s earliest example of this sense (*v.*, 4)
306 *wards* guards, postures of defence

288 *be* ed. (by Q1). All editors follow Q1, though the emendation is made in MS in the Harvard copy of the first issue. Sampson sought to evade the problem by glossing *accessary* as 'participation', for which there is no authority. Cf. Rowley's use of *be accessary* at IV, iv, 185 and in *All's Lost by Lust*, II, vi, 178.
292 *new morris*. Russell will make Fitzallen dance after his tune.

Boldly to defend your wife and family,
To walk unmuffled, dreadless of these flesh-hooks,
Even in the daring'st streets through all the city;
But now I find you a loose prodigal,   310
A large unthrift.—A whole thousand pound!
Come from him, girl, his inside is not sound.

FITZALLEN

Sir, I am wronged: these are malicious plots
Of some obscure enemies that I have;
These debts are none of mine.

RUSSELL

                            Ay, all say so: 315
Perhaps you stand engaged for other men;
If so you do, you must then call't your own;
The like arrearage do I run into
Should I bail you; but I have vowed against it,
And I will keep my vows; that's religious.   320

FITZALLEN

All this is nothing so, sir.

RUSSELL

                    Nothing so?
By my faith, it is, sir; my vows are firm.

FITZALLEN

I neither owe these debts, nor engaged for others.

RUSSELL

The easier is your liberty regained;
These appear proofs to me.

COLONEL

                    Liberty, sir?   325
I hope you'll not see him go to prison.

RUSSELL

I do not mean to bear him company
So far, but I'll see him out of my doors.

308 *unmuffled* uncovered. Cf. IV, iv, 122
309 *daring'st streets* the most open parts of the city, where there was
   no right of sanctuary (Sampson)
313 lineation ed. (These . . . plots Q1 as separate line)
318 *arrearage* debt
323 lineation ed. (Nor . . . others Q1 as separate line)

308 *flesh-hooks*. Hooks for removing flesh from the pot. Flesh-hook is the
   name of a sergeant in Middleton's *Anything for a Quiet Life*.
323 *nor engaged*. 'Nor did I engage (myself)', a legitimate active use; cf. II,
   i, 212 and *OED*, *v.*, 6. Other editors supply 'am' or 'am I'.

Oh sir, let him go to prison; 'tis a school
To tame wild bloods, he'll be much better for't.   330
COLONEL
Better for lying in prison?
RUSSELL
                    In prison:
Believe it, many an honest man lies in prison,
Else all the keepers are knaves; they told me so themselves.
COLONEL
Sir, I do now suspect you have betrayed him,
And us, to cause us to be weaponless;   335
If it be so, y'are a blood-sucking churl,
One that was born in a great frost, when charity
Could not stir a finger; and you shall die
In heat of a burning fever i'th' dog-days
To begin your hell to you: I have said your grace for you,   340
Now get you to supper as soon as you can;
Pluto, the master of the house, is set already.
CAPTAIN AGER
Sir, you do wrong mine uncle.
COLONEL
                    Pox on your uncle
And all his kin, if my kinsman mingle
No blood with him!
CAPTAIN AGER
                    Y'are a foul-mouthed fellow.   345
COLONEL
Foul-mouthed I will be—th'art the son of a whore!

333 lineation ed. (They . . . themselues Q1 as separate line)
342 *set* seated (at table). Perhaps punning on *set* = 'prepared'

---

337 *great frost.* A reference to the Great Frost of 1607–08, during which the
    Thames was frozen for 6 weeks.
339 *dog-days.* The period of the year, usually dated from early July until
    around 11 August, thought the hottest and most unwholesome for
    Europeans.
346 *son . . . whore.* The standard formula for obtaining a challenge; cf.
    Shirley, *The Gamester*, I, i, p. 195: 'there's . . . A base and sordid
    provocation/Used among gentlemen; they cannot quarrel/About a glass
    of wine, but out flies straight,/*Son of a Whore*! Dead mothers must be
    torn/Out of their graves, or living have their names/Poison'd by a
    prodigious breath' (*Dramatic Works and Poems*, ed. W. Gifford, 6 vols.,
    1833).

CAPTAIN AGER

Ha! Whore? Plagues and furies! I'll thrust that back,
Or pluck thy heart out after! Son of a whore?

COLONEL

On thy life I'll prove it.

CAPTAIN AGER

                    Death, I am naked!
Uncle, I'll give you my left hand for my sword   350
To arm my right with!—Oh, this fire will flame me
Into present ashes!

COLONEL

                    Sir, give us weapons;
We ask our own; you will not rob us of them?

RUSSELL

No, sir, but still restrain your furies here;
At my door I'll give you them, nor at this time   355
My nephew's; a time will better suit you;
And I must tell you, sir, you have spoke swords,
And 'gainst the law of arms poisoned the blades,
And with them wounded the reputation
Of an unblemished woman. Would you were out of my doors!   360

COLONEL

Pox on your doors, and let it run all your house o'er!
Give me my sword!

CAPTAIN AGER

                    We shall meet, Colonel?

COLONEL

Yes, better provided: to spur thee more,
I do repeat my words—son of a whore! *Exit with his* FRIEND

349 *naked* unarmed
352 *present* instant

---

357 *spoke swords.* A stock metaphor; cf. *Hamlet*, III, ii, 386; *Much Ado About Nothing*, II, i, 223. Here it takes on additional meaning, since Russell is implying that the insult has made a duel inevitable: Bowers quotes James I's MS 'Treatise against Duelling': 'imputation of incontinencie to women ... [duellists] conceaue irreparable by any other meane then the sworde' ('Duelling Code', 47).
361 *Pox ... o'er.* A literal use of the standard curse. The reference is to plague marks daubed on the doors of infected houses.
364 *repeat my words.* This flouts the laws of duello and seriously damages the Colonel's cause: 'After that one hath called the other to the battel ... it is not lawful that either may offend his aduersarie anie more ... this censure is ... vniuersally approued' (Saviolo, *Practice*, sig. X4^r).

CAPTAIN'S FRIEND

    Come, sir, 'tis no worse than 'twas; you can do nothing now. 365
                         Exit CAPTAIN *and his* FRIEND

RUSSELL

    No, I'll bar him now.—Away with that beggar!   *Exit*

JANE

    Good sir, let this persuade you for two minutes' stay;
                         [*Gives money*]
    At this price, I know, you can wait all day.

1 SERGEANT

    You know the remora that stays our ship always.

JANE

    Your ship sinks many when this hold lets go.—   370
    Oh my Fitzallen, what is to be done?

FITZALLEN

    To be still thine is all my part to be,
    Whether in freedom or captivity.

JANE

    But art thou so engaged as this pretends?

FITZALLEN

    By heaven, sweet Jane, 'tis all a hellish plot: 375
    Your cruel-smiling father all this while
    Has candied o'er a bitter pill for me,
    Thinking by my remove to plant some other
    And then let go his fangs.

JANE

               Plant some other?
    Thou hast too firmly stamped me for thine own   380
    Ever to be rased out: I am not current
    In any other's hand; I fear too soon
    I shall discover it.

FITZALLEN

             Let come the worst;

---

365 lineation ed. (You . . . now Q1 as separate line)
372 *still* always
374 *pretends* claims
380–2 *Thou . . . hand* the metaphor is from coinage
383 *discover* reveal

---

369 *remora*. It was believed that the remora could stay the course of any
    ship to which it attached itself.
377 *candied . . . pill*. Cf. the proverbs 'To sugar the pill' and 'To swallow a
    bitter pill' (Tilley, P325–6).

Bind but this knot with an unloosed line,
I will be still thine own.

JANE
                    And I'll be thine.   385

1 SERGEANT
My watch has gone two minutes, master.

FITZALLEN
It shall not be renewed; I go, sir.—Farewell!

JANE
Farewell; we both are prisoned, though not together;
But here's the difference in our luckless chance:
I fear mine own, wish thy deliverance.   390

FITZALLEN
Our hearts shall hourly visit: I'll send to thee;
Then 'tis no prison where the mind is free.

                    Exit FITZALLEN *with* OFFICERS

                    Enter RUSSELL

RUSSELL
So, let him go.—Now, wench, I bring thee joys,
A fair sunshine after this angry storm.
It was my policy to remove this beggar: 395
What? shall rich men wed their only daughters
To two fair suits of clothes, and perhaps yet
The poor taylor is unpaid? No, no, my girl,
I have a lad of thousands coming in.
Suppose he have more wealth than wit to guide it;   400
Why, there's thy gains: thou keep'st the keys of all,
Disposest all; and for generation,
Man does most seldom stamp 'em from the brain:

---

384 *unloosed* unloosened   385 *still* always
394 *storm* cf. I, i, 137–8, 182–3; III, i, 66–9   395 *policy* stratagem

---

384 *knot.* i.e., love-knot, a familiar idea; cf. *The Family of Love*, I, ii, 130–1:
'Be thou as loyal as I constant prove,/And time shall knit our mutual
knot of love'.
386 *master.* Q1 reads 'M.' which could equally well be short for 'mistress'.
As Fitzallen replies, I follow Dyce.
392 *'tis . . . free.* Probably proverbial (cf. Tilley, M972, 'My mind to me a
kingdom is'), though Sampson suggests that Milton remembered the
line in *Paradise Lost*, i, 254–9. The mind's superior detachment from
the external world was a standard idea of the stoics.
401–2 *thou . . . all.* A stock expression; cf. *The Puritan*, I, i, 109–10: 'I had
keyes of all, kept all, receiu'd all'.

Wise men begets fools, and fools are the fathers
To many wise children. *Histeron proteron*,   405
A great scholar may beget an idiot,
And from the plough-tail may come a great scholar;
Nay, they are frequent propagations.

JANE

I am not well, sir.

RUSSELL

               Ha! not well, my girl?
Thou shalt have a physician then,   410
The best that gold can fetch upon his foot-cloth.
Thou knowest my tender pity to thee ever;
Want nothing that thy wishes can instruct thee
To call for.—'Fore me, and thou look'st half-ill indeed!
But I'll bring one within a day to thee   415
Shall rouse thee up; for he's come up already,
One Master Chough, a Cornish gentleman;
H'as as much land of his own fee-simple
As a crow can fly over in half a day;
And now I think on't, at the Crow at Aldgate   420
His lodging is. He shall so stir thee up!—
Come, come, be cheered; think of thy preferment:
Honour and attendance, these will bring thee health;
And the way to 'em is to climb by wealth.   *Exeunt*

---

405 *Histeron proteron* by an inversion of the natural order (*OED, sb.,* 3.c)

407 *plough-tail* i.e., farm-labour (a common expression)

414 *'Fore me* see I, i, 243

416 *come up* to London from the country

---

404 *begets.* Common form of the third person plural. See E. A. Abbott, *A Shakespearian Grammar*, 1875 edn., sec. 333.

411 *foot-cloth.* Ornamented cloth laid over the back of a horse or mule and hanging down to the ground on each side. Especially favoured by physicians as a sign of their professional eminence.

418 *fee-simple.* Belonging to him and his heirs forever; see P. S. Clarkson and C. T. Warren, *The Law of Property in Shakespeare and the Elizabethan Drama*, Baltimore, 1942, pp. 50–4.

420 *Crow.* No inn of this name in Aldgate is recorded, but John Taylor mentions 'the crowne without Algate' in *The Carriers' Cosmography*, 1637, sig. B1ᵛ. 'Crow' is clearly correct, however (though Sampson suggests emending to 'Crown'), since it follows from the previous line and was chosen as amusingly appropriate to the name of the lodger. Sugden's suggestion (p. 139) that the Crow was another name of the Magpie in Aldgate High Street is somewhat fanciful.

Act II, Scene i

Enter CAPTAIN AGER

CAPTAIN AGER
  The son of a whore?
  There is not such another murdering-piece
  In all the stock of calumny; it kills
  At one report two reputations,
  A mother's and a son's. If it were possible   5
  That souls could fight after the bodies fell,
  This were a quarrel for 'em; he should be one, indeed,
  That never heard of heaven's joys or hell's torments
  To fight this out. I am too full of conscience,
  Knowledge, and patience, to give justice to't;   10
  So careful of my eternity, which consists
  Of upright actions, that unless I knew
  It were a truth I stood for, any coward
  Might make my breast his footpace; and who lives
  That can assure the truth of his conception,   15
  More than a mother's carriage makes it hopeful?
  And is't not miserable valour then,
  That man should hazard all upon things doubtful?
  Oh, there's the cruelty of my foe's advantage!
  Could but my soul resolve my cause were just,   20
  Earth's mountain nor sea's surge should hide him from me;
  E'en to hell's threshold would I follow him,
  And see the slanderer in before I left him:
  But as it is, it fears me; and I never
  Appeared too conscionably just till now.   25

2 *murdering-piece* small but destructive piece of artillery which fired
  grape-shot. Cf. *Hamlet*, IV, v, 92
4 *report* (i) account, disclosure (ii) detonation
14 *footpace* step, platform   16 *carriage* conduct
24 *fears* frightens   25 *conscionably* conscientiously

---

9 *conscience.* Cf. *Hamlet*, III, i, 83: 'Thus conscience does make cowards
  of us all'.
12–13 *unless . . . for.* Bowers quotes an anonymous MS treatise against
  duelling: 'fear of damnation after fight in defence of bad quarrells will
  make men fearfull of vniust chalinge ore vntrue speakinge or putting
  their sowles in hasarde' ('Duelling Code', 53). Cf. ll.78–82.
18 *all.* i.e., his 'eternity'. Cf. *A Woman Killed with Kindness*, viii, 73–5: 'I
  durst pawn my life, and on their faith/Hazard the dear salvation of my
  soul,/Yet in my trust I may be too secure'.

My good opinion of her life and virtues
Bids me go on, and fain would I be ruled by't;
But when my judgement tells me she's but woman,
Whose frailty let in death to all mankind,
My valour shrinks at that. Certain she's good;   30
There only wants but my assurance in't,
And all things then were perfect. How I thirst for't!
Here comes the only she that could resolve—
But 'tis too vild a question to demand indeed.

Enter the LADY AGER

LADY AGER
Son, I've a suit to you.
CAPTAIN AGER [*Aside*]
                That may do well.—   35
To me, good madam? You're most sure to speed in't,
Be't i' my power to grant it.
LADY AGER
              'Tis my love
Makes the request: that you would never part
From England more.
CAPTAIN AGER
          With all my heart 'tis granted.—
[*Aside*] I'm sure I'm i'th' way never to part from't.   40
LADY AGER
Where left you your dear friend the Colonel?
CAPTAIN AGER
Oh, the dear Colonel—I should meet him soon.
LADY AGER
Oh fail him not then! He's a gentleman
The fame and reputation of your time
Is much engaged to.
CAPTAIN AGER
         Yes, and you knew all, mother.   45
LADY AGER
I thought I'd known so much of his fair goodness,
More could not have been looked for.

---

29 *frailty* ed. (fraileto Q1 frailtie to Q2)   34 *vild* vile   45 *and* if

28–9 *But . . . mankind.* Comments on the folly of a man staking his honour
    on a woman's faith are common, though especially frequent in
    Middleton. Cf. Hamlet's 'Frailty, thy name is woman' (I, ii, 146).
35–40 *Son . . . from't.* Possibly a reminiscence of *Hamlet*, I, ii, 118–20.

CAPTAIN AGER
                              Oh, yes, yes, madam,
And this his last exceeded all the rest.
LADY AGER
For gratitude's sake, let me know this, I prithee.
CAPTAIN AGER
Then thus; and I desire your censure freely,   50
Whether it appeared not a strange noble kindness in him.
LADY AGER
Trust me, I long to hear't.
CAPTAIN AGER
                              You know he's hasty—
That by the way.
LADY AGER
                    So are the best conditions;
Your father was the like.
CAPTAIN AGER [*Aside*]
                              I begin now
To doubt me more: why am not I so too then?   55
Blood follows blood through forty generations,
And I've a slow-paced wrath—a shrewd dilemma!
LADY AGER
Well, as you were saying, sir.
CAPTAIN AGER
                              Marry, thus, good madam:
There was in company a foul-mouthed villain—stay, stay,
Who should I liken him to that you have seen?   60
He comes so near one that I would not match him with—
Faith, just o'th' Colonel's pitch. He's ne'er the worse man;
Usurers have been compared to magistrates,
Extortioners to lawyers, and the like,
But they all prove ne'er the worse men for that.   65
LADY AGER
That's bad enough; they need not.
CAPTAIN AGER
                              This rude fellow,

50 *censure* judgement
53 *conditions* dispositions
57 *slow-paced OED* cites no such usage before 1648 (*a.*, 1)
    shrewd cruel, severe

62 *pitch*. Rank, status (*OED*, *sb.*, 22). Other editors gloss 'height' (*sb.*, 20),
    but it is clear from the next three lines that the comparison is one of
    social standing.

A shame to all humanity or manners,
Breathes from the rottenness of his gall and malice
The foulest stain that ever man's fame blemished;
Part of which fell upon your honour, madam,   70
Which heightened my affliction.

LADY AGER

                    Mine? My honour, sir?

CAPTAIN AGER

The Colonel, soon enraged—as he's all touchwood—
Takes fire before me, makes the quarrel his,
Appoints the field; my wrath could not be heard,
His was so high-pitched, so gloriously mounted.   75
Now what's the friendly fear that fights within me,
Should his brave noble fury undertake
A cause that were unjust in our defence,
And so to lose him everlastingly
In that dark depth where all bad quarrels sink,   80
Never to rise again. What pity 'twere
First to die here, and never to die there!

LADY AGER

Why, what's the quarrel—speak, sir—that should raise
Such fearful doubt, my honour bearing part on't?
The words, whate'er they were.

CAPTAIN AGER

                    Son of a whore.   85

LADY AGER

Thou liest!   *Strikes him*
And were my love ten thousand times more to thee,
Which is as much now as e'er mother's was,
So thou shouldst feel my anger. Dost thou call
That quarrel doubtful? Where are all my merits?   90
Not one stand up to tell this man his error?

72 lineation ed. (As . . . touch-wood Q1 as separate line)
    touchwood wood that is easily kindled, tinder: thus, 'hasty' (l.52).
    According to *OED*, here first used figuratively
86–7 one line in Q1

75 *high-pitched*. This looks backward and forward: (i) shrill, loud (ii) lofty.
86 s.d. Follows 1.90 in Q1. Dyce's relocation creates a far more powerful
    expression of Lady Ager's sense of outrage. The cramped appearance
    of the quarto page suggests that the direction was crowded out of its
    correct position.

Thou might'st as well bring the sun's truth in question
As thy birth or my honour!

CAPTAIN AGER

                          Now blessings crown you for't!
It is the joyfull'st blow that e'er flesh felt.

LADY AGER

Nay, stay, stay, sir; thou art not left so soon: 95
This is no question to be slighted off,
And at your pleasure closed up fair again,
As though you'd never touched it; no, honour doubted
Is honour deeply wounded; and it rages
More than a common smart, being of thy making.   100
For thee to fear my truth, it kills my comfort:
Where should fame seek for her reward, when he
That is her own by the great tie of blood
Is fardest off in bounty? Oh poor goodness,
That only pay'st thyself with thy own works,   105
For nothing else looks towards thee. Tell me pray,
Which of my loving cares dost thou requite
With this vild thought? which of my prayers or wishes?
Many thou owest me for; this seven year hast thou known me
A widow, only married to my vow;   110
That's no small witness of my faith and love

---

96 *slighted off* cast off disdainfully
97 *closed up* settled
104 *fardest* farthest
    bounty (i) munificence (ii) worth, nobility

---

92 *sun.* A regular touchstone for truth; cf. *A Midsummer Night's Dream*,
   III, ii, 50 and the proverb 'As clear as the sun' (Tilley, S969).
101 *truth.* In the wide sense of Chaucer's 'Trouthe is the hyeste thyng that
   man may kepe' (*The Franklin's Tale*, l.1479). A woman's truth was
   primarily represented by her chastity; cf. *A Woman Killed with
   Kindness*, iv, 11–12: 'a chaste and loving wife,/Perfection all, all truth'.
110 *vow.* i.e., marriage vow; cf. *Hamlet*, III, ii, 216–18. 17th-century
   disapproval of a widow who remarried was largely theoretical: a
   Jacobean audience would have admired Lady Ager as the follower of a
   noble ideal which sheer impracticability prevented most women from
   attaining. Such an ideal is at home in the main plot, which is concerned
   with codes of behaviour irrespective of circumstances. In the practical
   world of the subplot it would be out of place: 'a month's constancy/Is
   held a virtue in a city widow' (*More Dissemblers*, I, i, 13–14). See F. W.
   Wadsworth, 'Webster's *Duchess of Malfi* in the Light of Some
   Contemporary Ideas on Marriage and Remarriage', *PQ*, 35 (1956),
   394–407.

To him that in life was thy honoured father;
And live I now to know that good mistrusted?
CAPTAIN AGER
No, 't shall appear that my belief is cheerful,
For never was a mother's reputation 115
Noblier defended; 'tis my joy and pride
I have a firm to bestow upon it.
LADY AGER
What's that you said, sir?
CAPTAIN AGER
'Twere too bold and soon yet
To crave forgiveness of you: I will earn it first;
Dead or alive, I know I shall enjoy it. 120
LADY AGER
What's all this, sir?
CAPTAIN AGER
My joy's beyond expression!
I do but think how wretched I had been
Were this another's quarrel, and not mine.
LADY AGER
Why, is it yours?
CAPTAIN AGER
Mine? Think me not so miserable,
Not to be mine; then were I worse than abject, 125
More to be loathed than vileness or sin's dunghill.
Nor did I fear your goodness, faithful madam,
But came with greedy joy to be confirmed in't,
To give the nobler onset: then shines valour,
And admiration from her fixed sphere draws, 130
When it comes burnished with a righteous cause;
Without which I'm ten fadoms under coward,
That now am ten degrees above a man,
Which is but one of virtue's easiest wonders.

127 *fear* doubt
132 *fadoms* fathoms

---

117 *firm.* The line is ambiguous, but it is not necessary to emend, as do other editors, to 'firmness' or 'firm faith'. Either *belief* (l.114) is understood, or Middleton intends the noun meaning 'signature'.

129–31 *then . . . cause.* The sense is clear, though the cosmology (involving the sun drawing a fixed star from its sphere) is imperfect. Cf. *Much Ado*, V, i, 120: 'In a false quarrel there is no true valour'.

LADY AGER

But pray, stay; all this while I understood you   135
The Colonel was the man.

CAPTAIN AGER

Yes, he's the man;
The man of injury, reproach, and slander,
Which I must turn into his soul again.

LADY AGER

The Colonel do't? That's strange.

CAPTAIN AGER

The villain did it:
That's not so strange.—Your blessing and your leave.   140

LADY AGER

Come, come, you shall not go.

CAPTAIN AGER

Not go? Were death
Sent now to summon me to my eternity,
I'd put him off an hour! Why, the whole world
Has not chains strong enough to bind me from't:
The strongest is my reverence to you,   145
Which if you force upon me in this case,
I must be forced to break it.

LADY AGER

Stay, I say!

CAPTAIN AGER

In anything command me but in this, madam.

LADY AGER

[*Aside*] 'Las, I shall lose him!—You'll hear me first.

CAPTAIN AGER

At my return I will.   150

LADY AGER

You'll never hear me more, then.

CAPTAIN AGER

How?

135 *understood you* understood that

---

138 *turn into.* Often used in flinging back an insult; cf. *Richard II*, IV, i,
39–40: 'I will turn thy falsehood to thy heart . . . with my rapier's
point'. 'Soul' rather than the conventional 'heart' or 'throat' stresses
Ager's religious preoccupations.

151 *You'll . . . then.* The prediction concerns the traditional belief in the
providential victory of justice in the trial by combat, often cited by
supporters of the duello. It thus entails the truth of the Colonel's
aspersion. Cf. III, i, 165–6.

LADY AGER
  Come back, I say!
  You may well think there's cause I call so often.
CAPTAIN AGER
  Ha, cause? what cause?   155
LADY AGER
  So much, you must not go.
CAPTAIN AGER
  How?
LADY AGER
  You must not go.
CAPTAIN AGER
  Must not? Why?
LADY AGER
             I know a reason for't,
  Which I could wish you'd yield to, and not know;   160
  If not, it must come forth. Faith, do not know,
  And yet obey my will.
CAPTAIN AGER
               Why, I desire
  To know no other than the cause I have,
  Nor should you wish it, if you take your injury;
  For one more great I know the world includes not.   165
LADY AGER
  Yes, one that makes this nothing.—Yet be ruled,
  And if you understand not, seek no further.
CAPTAIN AGER
  I must, for this is nothing.
LADY AGER
             Then take all;
  And if amongst it you receive that secret
  That will offend you, though you condemn me,   170
  Yet blame yourself a little; for perhaps
  I would have made my reputation sound
  Upon another's hazard with less pity;
  But upon yours I dare not.
CAPTAIN AGER
             How?

---

157 *How* What? (exclamation of surprise)
164 *take . . . injury* either 'consider your injury' or 'accept that you
    have been injured'

LADY AGER

                        I dare not.
'Twas your own seeking, this.

CAPTAIN AGER

                        If you mean evilly,   175
I cannot understand you; nor for all the riches
This life has, would I.

LADY AGER

                  Would you never might!

CAPTAIN AGER

Why, your goodness, that I joy to fight for.

LADY AGER

In that you neither right your joy nor me.

CAPTAIN AGER

What an ill orator has virtue got here!   180
Why, shall I dare to think it a thing possible
That you were ever false?

LADY AGER

                Oh, fearfully!
As much as you come to.

CAPTAIN AGER

              Oh silence, cover me!
I've felt a deadlier wound than man can give me.—False?

LADY AGER

I was betrayed to a most sinful hour   185
By a corrupted soul I put in trust once,
A kinswoman.

CAPTAIN AGER

         Where is she? Let me pay her!

LADY AGER

Oh, dead long since.

CAPTAIN AGER

        Nay then, sh'as all her wages.—

---

182 *fearfully* to a fearful degree. *OED* cites no such usage before 1838 (*adv.*, 2)

177–8 Other editors make no comment, but at least one line of text seems to have dropped out here. Lady Ager must say something like 'What cause can you hope to right in this quarrel?'.

183 *As . . . to*. 'As much as *you* amount to', informing Ager that he is the offspring of the adultery (and thus literally the 'son of a whore').

188 *dead . . . wages.* 'The wages of sin is death' (Romans vi. 23).

False? Do not say't, for honour's goodness, do not!
You never could be so. He I called father   190
Deserved you at your best, when youth and merit
Could boast at highest in you; y'ad no grace
Or virtue that he matched not, no delight
That you invented but he sent it crowned
To your full-wishing soul.

LADY AGER

                    That heaps my guiltiness.   195

CAPTAIN AGER

Oh, were you so unhappy to be false,
Both to yourself and me?—but to me chiefly:
What a day's hope is here lost, and with it
The joys of a just cause! Had you but thought
On such a noble quarrel, you'd ha' died   200
Ere you'd ha' yielded—for the sin's hate first,
Next for the shame of this hour's cowardice.
Cursed be the heat that lost me such a cause,
A work that I was made for! Quench, my spirit,
And out with honour's flaming lights within thee!   205
Be dark and dead to all respects of manhood!
I never shall have use of valour more.
Put off your vow, for shame! Why should you hoard up
Such justice for a barren widowhood,
That was so injurious to the faith of wedlock?   *Exit* LADY   210
I should be dead, for all my life's work's ended;
I dare not fight a stroke now, nor engage
The noble resolution of my friends;

        Enter two FRIENDS *of* CAPTAIN AGER'*s*

That were more vild.—They're here; kill me, my shame!
I am not for the fellowship of honour.   215

1 CAPTAIN'S FRIEND

Captain! fie, come, sir; we have been seeking for you

---

194 *crowned* worthily completed (*OED*, *v.*, 11), complementing 'invented'
195 *full-wishing* earnestly desiring (?). Not in *OED*
196 *unhappy* ill-fated
203 *heat* sexual excitement. Cf. *Much Ado About Nothing*, IV, i, 40
204 *Quench* used intransitively
208 *Put off* renounce

189–97 *False . . . chiefly*. Cf. *Hamlet*, I, ii, 137–45 and III, iv (the closet scene).

Very late today. This was not wont to be;
Your enemy's i'th' field.

CAPTAIN AGER [*Aside*]
               Truth enters cheerfully.

2 CAPTAIN'S FRIEND
Good faith, sir, y'ave a royal quarrel on't.

CAPTAIN AGER
Yes, in some other country, Spain or Italy,   220
It would be held so.

1 CAPTAIN'S FRIEND
            How? And is't not here so?

CAPTAIN AGER
'Tis not so contumeliously received
In these parts, and you mark it.

1 CAPTAIN'S FRIEND
                Not in these?
Why, prithee, what is more, or can be?

CAPTAIN AGER
                     Yes,
That ordinary commotioner, the lie,   225
Is father of most quarrels in this climate,
And held here capital, and you go to that.

2 CAPTAIN'S FRIEND
But, sir, I hope you will not go to that,
Or change your own for it. 'Son of a whore'—
Why, there's the lie down to posterity,   230
The lie to birth, the lie to honesty.
Why would you cozen yourself so, and beguile

223 *and* if
225 *commotioner* disturber, trouble-maker
226 *climate* region
229 *your own* your own quarrel
232 *cozen* cheat
     beguile foil, disappoint

---

218 s.d. Other editors fail to supply the direction, but the alternative is
     Ager's clear admission of his mother's unchastity. In this scene Q1
     lacks the same direction at ll. 35, 40, 54, and 149.
220 *Spain . . . Italy*. Nations thought particularly sensitive about questions
     of honour.
225 *the lie*. Neither party had given the other the lie during the quarrel.
227 *capital*. All authorities on the managing of quarrels stressed that the
     deadliness of the lie made combat unavoidable. Cf. Ralegh's poem, 'The
     Lie', ll.75–6: 'to giue the lie,/Deserues no lesse than stabbing'.

So brave a cause, manhood's best masterpiece?
Do you ever hope for one so brave again?
CAPTAIN AGER
Consider then the man, Colonel,   235
Exactly worthy, absolutely noble,
However spleen and rage abuses him;
And 'tis not well nor manly to pursue
A man's infirmity.
1 CAPTAIN'S FRIEND
               Oh miracle!
So hopeful, valiant, and complete a captain   240
Possessed with a tame devil!—Come out! Thou spoilest
The most improved young soldier of seven kingdoms:
Made captain at nineteen, which was deserved
The year before, but honour comes behind still.
Come out, I say! This was not wont to be;   245
That spirit never stood in need of provocation,
Nor shall it now. Away, sir!
CAPTAIN AGER
                Urge me not.
1 CAPTAIN'S FRIEND
By manhood's reverend honour, but we must!
CAPTAIN AGER
I will not fight a stroke.
1 CAPTAIN'S FRIEND
              Oh blasphemy
To sacred valour!
CAPTAIN AGER
           Lead me where you list.   250
1 CAPTAIN'S FRIEND
Pardon this traitorous slumber, clogged with evils:
Give captains rather wives than such tame devils!   *Exeunt*

233 *masterpiece* chief excellence (*OED, sb.,* 2)
236 *Exactly* perfectly, completely
240 *complete* perfect
244 *still* always
252 *wives* proleptic irony

---

235 *Colonel.* Previous editors supply 'the', but cf. I, i, 27 and the similar
    usage in *More Dissemblers,* III, i, 218–19: 'Duchess and I were a fit
    match'.
241 *Come out.* As if exorcizing the devil (Sampson). Cf. Luke viii. 29.

[Act II, Scene ii]

Enter PHYSICIAN *and* JANE

PHYSICIAN
  Nay, mistress, you must not be covered to me;
  The patient must ope to the physician
  All her dearest sorrows; art is blinded else,
  And cannot show her mystical effects.
JANE
  Can art be so dim-sighted, learned sir?   5
  I did not think her so incapacious.
  You train me, as I guess, like a conjuror,
  One of our fine oraculous wizards,
  Who, from the help of his examinant,
  By the near guess of his suspicion,   10
  Appoints out the thief by the marks he tells him.
  Have you no skill in physiognomy?
  What colour, says your coat, is my disease?
  I am unmarried, and it cannot be yellow;
  If it be maiden green, you cannot miss it.   15

  1 *covered* secretive
  6 *incapacious* unable to apprehend. *OED*'s first example of this
    sense (*a.*, 2)
  7 *train* lure
  8 *fine* ed. (fiue Q1)
    oraculous speaking in the manner of an oracle
  9 *examinant* one who is being examined (the opposite of the modern
    meaning)
  13 *coat* i.e., profession. Cf. *Measure for Measure*, IV, ii, 180
  14 *yellow* the colour of jealousy

  1 *mistress*. Q1 reads 'Master', the compositor's erroneous expansion of
    the abbreviation 'M.' in his copy. Cf. I, i, 386 and note.
  8 *oraculous wizards*. 'Of the magical functions performed by the cunning
    men and wise women . . . [one of] the most common seems to have
    been the detection of theft and the recovery of stolen goods' (K.
    Thomas, *Religion and the Decline of Magic*, 1971, pp. 212–13). Cf.
    Heywood's *The Wise Woman of Hogsdon*, whose wise woman operates
    precisely in the way Jane describes.
  11 *Appoints*. 'Points', to which all editors mistakenly emend; cf. *approve*
    = 'prove'.
  15 *maiden green*. Referring to green-sickness or chlorosis, 'an anaemic
    sickness of young women (with consequent greenish complexion)';
    thought 'a sign of a girl's love-sickness, or of vague desire, for a man'
    (Partridge, p. 117).

PHYSICIAN
    I cannot see that vacuum in your blood;
    But, gentlewoman, if you love yourself,
    Love my advice; be free and plain with me:
    Where lies your grief?
JANE
               Where lies my grief indeed?
    I cannot tell the truth where my grief lies,   20
    But my joy's imprisoned.
PHYSICIAN
               This is mystical.
JANE
    Lord, what plain questions you make problems of!
    Your art is such a regular highway
    That, put you out of it, and you are lost.
    My heart is imprisoned in my body, sir;   25
    There's all my joy; and my sorrow too
    Lies very near it.
PHYSICIAN
            They are bad adjuncts;
    Your joy and grief, lying so near together,
    Can propagate no happy issue: remove
    The one, and let it be the worst—your grief—   30
    If you'll propose the best unto your joy.
JANE
    Why, now comes your skill: what physic for it?
PHYSICIAN
    Now I have found you out: you are in love.
JANE
    I think I am: what's your appliance now?
    Can all your Paracelsian mixtures cure it?   35

16 *vacuum* emptiness, thinness. Referring to the supposed cause of
    anaemia
20 *lies* punning on 'tells lies'
34 *what's* Q2 (what Q1)
    appliance application, treatment

19–27 *Where . . . it.* Jane's equivocal replies concern her unborn child (her
    grief and *sorrow*) and the plight of Fitzallen (her *joy* and *heart*); cf. I, i,
    391.
35 *Paracelsian.* Theophrastus of Hohenheim (1493–1541), better known as
    Paracelsus, was the first to introduce chemistry to the science of
    medicine. According to *OED*, the first occurrence of the adjective.

'Tmust be a surgeon of the civil law,
I fear, that must cure me.
PHYSICIAN
                        Gentlewoman,
If you knew well my heart, you would not be
So circular; the very common name
Of physician might reprove your niceness: 40
We are as secret as your confessors,
And as firm obliged; 'tis a fine like death
For us to blab.
JANE
              I will trust you; yet, sir,
I had rather do it by attorney to you:
I else have blushes that will stop my tongue.   45
Have you no friend so friendly as yourself
Of mine own sex, to whom I might impart
My sorrows to you at the second hand?
PHYSICIAN
Why, law, there I hit you! and be confirmed,
I'll give you such a bosom counsellor,   50
That your own tongue shall be sooner false to you.
Make yourself unready, and be naked to her;
I'll fetch her presently.   *Exit* PHYSICIAN
JANE
                I must reveal;
My shame will else take tongue, and speak before me;
'Tis a necessity impulsive drives me.   55
Oh my hard fate!—but my more hard father,
That father of my fate:—a father, said I?
What a strange paradox I run into!

39 *very common name* familiar name alone
40 *niceness* coyness
42 *obliged* bound by duty
49 *law* see I, i, 182
    hit reach, succeed with
53 *presently* at once

41–3 *We . . . blab.* Cf. the well-known clause in the Hippocratic Oath: 'Whatsoeuer during the tyme of any cure I shall either see or heare . . . such as requireth secresie and silence, I shal not vtter nor bewray to any maner of person' (T. Newton, *The Old Man's Dietary*, 1586, sig. D4r). The 'fine' would be imposed by the Royal College of Physicians.
52 *Make . . . unready.* 'Undress yourself', here metaphorical: the line means 'stop equivocating and speak openly to her'.

I must accuse two fathers of my fate
And fault, a reciprocal generation: 60
The father of my fault would have repaired
His faulty issue, but my fate's father hinders it:
Then fate and fault, wherever I begin,
I must blame both, and yet 'twas love did sin.

Enter PHYSICIAN *and* ANNE, *his sister*

PHYSICIAN
   Look you, mistress, here's your closet; put in   65
   What you please, you ever keep the key of it.
JANE
   Let me speak private, sir.
PHYSICIAN
                    With all my heart;
   I will be more than mine ears' length from you. [*Withdraws*]
JANE
   You hold some endeared place with this gentleman?
ANNE
   He's my brother, forsooth, I his creature;   70
   He does command me any lawful office,
   Either in act or counsel.
JANE
                    I must not doubt you;
   Your brother has protested secrecy,
   And strengthened me in you. I must lay ope
   A guilty sorrow to you: I am with child.   75
   'Tis no black swan I show you; these spots stick
   Upon the face of many go for maids.
   I that had face enough to do the deed,
   Cannot want tongue to speak it; but 'tis to you,
   Whom I accept my helper.
ANNE
                    Mistress, 'tis locked   80

69 *endeared* dear. *OED* cites no such usage before 1841 (*ppl. a.*, 2)
70 *creature* instrument, subordinate
76 *spots* pun on *spot* = (i) facial (ii) moral blemish

65–6 *here's . . . it.* A stock expression; cf. *Hamlet*, I, iii, 85–6 and *A
    Shoemaker, a Gentleman*, I, iii, 48: 'You have lockt the Closset and
    keepe the Key of it'.
76 *no black swan.* Nothing extraordinary. A stock phrase originating in
    Juvenal's assertion that a chaste wife is a *rara avis in terris nigroque
    simillima cycno* (Satire VI, l.165).

Within a castle that's invincible:
It is too late to wish it were undone.

JANE
I have scarce a wish within myself so strong,
For, understand me, 'tis not all so ill
As you may yet conceit it: this deed was done   85
When heaven had witness to the jugal knot;
Only the barren ceremony wants,
Which by an adverse father is abridged.

ANNE
Would my pity could help you.

JANE
                                              Your counsel may.
My father yet shoots widest from my sorrow,   90
And, with a care indulgent, seeing me changed
From what I was, sends for your good brother
To find my grief, and practise remedy.
You know it, give it him; but if a fourth
Be added to this counsel, I will say   95
Ye're worse than you can call me at the worst,
At this advantage of my reputation.

ANNE
I will revive a reputation
That women long has lost: I'll keep counsel.
I'll only now oblige my teeth to you,   100
And they shall bite the blabber, if it offer
To breathe on an offending syllable.

---

85 *yet conceit* still believe
86 *jugal* conjugal
88 *abridged* debarred
99 *has* see I, i, 404 and note
100 *oblige . . . to you* pledge in your service

85–8 *this . . . abridged.* Cf. Claudio's 'she is fast my wife,/Save that we do
the denunciation lack/Of outward order' (*Measure for Measure*, I, i,
157–9). Both couples have contracted a *de praesenti* betrothal, which
was regarded as legally binding. D. P. Harding shows that cohabitation
on the basis of such a contract was unlikely to have been thought sinful
by contemporary audiences ('Elizabethan Betrothals and *Measure for
Measure*', *JEGP*, 49 (1950), 139–58). Middleton's *The Witch*, IV, ii,
7–17 summarizes the prevailing attitude.
90 *shoots widest.* Is farthest from realizing. Another of Rowley's archery
metaphors; cf. *A New Wonder*, IV, i, p. 165.

JANE

I trust you; go, whisper; here comes my father.

Enter RUSSELL, CHOUGH, *and* TRIMTRAM

RUSSELL

Sir, you are welcome; more, and most welcome:
All the degrees of welcome: thrice welcome, sir.   105
CHOUGH

Is this your daughter, sir?
RUSSELL

Mine only joy, sir.
CHOUGH

I'll show her the Cornish hug, sir.—[*Embraces* JANE] I have
kissed you now, sweetheart, and I never do any kindness to
my friends but I use to hit 'em in the teeth with it presently.
TRIMTRAM

My name is Trimtram, forsooth: look, what my master does,   110
I use to do the like. [*Offers to embrace* ANNE]
ANNE

You are deceived, sir; I am not this gentlewoman's servant,
to make your courtesy equal.
CHOUGH

You do not know me, mistress?
JANE

No indeed.—[*Aside*] I doubt I shall learn too soon.   115
CHOUGH

My name is Chough, a Cornish gentleman; my man's mine

109 *presently* at once
115 *doubt* fear

---

107 *Cornish hug.* In Cornish wrestling, the preliminary stance at the
beginning of a bout, each wrestler holding the other's clothing (one of
the rules cited by Carew, *The Survey of Cornwall*, f. 76ʳ, is 'wearing a
girdle to take hold by'). *OED*'s earliest example of the term.
108–9 *I never . . . presently.* A joking allusion to another sense of 'Cornish
hug': 'It is figuratively appliable to the deceitfull dealing of such, who
secretly design their overthrow, whom they openly embrace' (T. Fuller,
The History of the Worthies of England, 1662, 'Cornwall', p. 198).
110–11 *My . . . like.* Trimtram's name, and his copying of Chough, are
explained by the proverb 'Trim tram, like master, like man' (Tilley,
T525). Perhaps also intended is 'a parody of *Tristram*, the Cornish
knight equally distinguished for valour and amorousness' (Power, op.
cit., 140).

own countryman too, i'faith. I warrant you took us for some
of the small islanders.

JANE

I did indeed, between the Scotch and Irish.

CHOUGH

Red-shanks? I thought so, by my truth. No, truly, we are right   120
Cornish diamonds.

TRIMTRAM

Yes, we cut out quarrels, and break glasses, where we go.

PHYSICIAN

[*Aside to* ANNE] If it be hidden from her father, yet
His ignorance understands well his knowledge,
For this I guess to be some rich coxcomb   125
He'd put upon his daughter.

ANNE

                    That's plainly so.

PHYSICIAN

Then only she's beholding to our help
For the close delivery of her burden,
Else all's overthrown.

ANNE

                    And pray be faithful in that, sir.

PHYSICIAN

Tush, we physicians are the truest   130
Alchemists, that from the ore and dross of sin
Can new distil a maidenhead again.

RUSSELL

How do you like her, sir?

CHOUGH

Troth, I do like her, sir, in the way of comparison, to any-

---

127 *beholding* common in early 17th century for 'beholden'
128 *close* secret
131 *dross* scum thrown off from metals in the process of melting
134 *like* punning on 'liken'

---

120 *Red-shanks*. Term of contempt for Scottish Highlanders and native
Irish (Bullen). Glancing ironically at Chough himself, since the red-
shank was another red-legged sea-bird common in Cornwall (see p. 5).
121 *Cornish diamonds*. Cornish rock-crystal. The comparison is (unintentionally) invidious, for the term was a by-word for fraudulence; cf. B.
Rich, *My Lady's Looking-Glass*, 1616, p. 53: 'a malecontent, a right
cornish Diamond, that although a *counterfeit*, would yet be set in gold'.
122 *cut ... quarrels*. (i) pick quarrels (ii) cut out panes of glass (usually
diamond-shaped).

thing that a man would desire; I am as high as the Mount in   135
love with her already, and that's as far as I can go by land;
but I hope to go further by water with her one day.

RUSSELL

I tell you, sir, she has lost some colour
By wrestling with a peevish sickness now of late.

CHOUGH

Wrestle? Nay, and she love wrestling, I'll teach her a trick   140
to overthrow any peevish sickness in London, whate'er it be.

RUSSELL

Well, she had a rich beauty, though I say't;
Nor is it lost: a little thing repairs it.

CHOUGH

She shall command the best thing that I have in Middlesex,
i'faith.   145

RUSSELL

Well, sir, talk with her, give her a relish
Of your good liking to her; you shall have time
And free access to finish what you now begin.

JANE

[*Aside*] What means my father? My love's unjust restraint,
My shame, were it published, both together   150
Could not afflict me like this odious fool.
Now I see why he hated my Fitzallen.

CHOUGH

Sweet lady, your father says you are a wrestler: if you love
that sport, I love you the better; i'faith, I love it as well as
I love my meat after supper; 'tis indeed meat, drink, and   155
cloth to me.

---

139 *peevish* tiresome   140 *and* if
146 *relish* foretaste   155 *meat* food

135–6 *I . . . land*. St Michael's Mount stands in Mount's Bay near Land's
   End, and is connected to the mainland only at low water. Hence often
   cited as an ultimate point; cf. Donne, Satire II, ll.76–7: 'all our
   land . . . from Mount, to Dover Strand'.
137 *water*. Punning on water = 'semen'; cf. *The Roaring Girl*, IV, ii, 78.
140 *Wrestle*. Besides their function as slapstick, Chough's antics allow
   Rowley to ring the changes on the bawdy sense of *wrestle*, 'to be one of
   two contenders in a love-bout' (Partridge, *s.v.*).
143 *little thing*. Double-edged irony. Russell is slyly hinting at Chough's
   wealth (cf. I, i, 423–4), but the audience can also apply his remark to
   Jane's baby.
144 *Middlesex*. A broad sexual pun. Place-name quibbles are one of
   Rowley's trade-marks; cf. l.191, IV, iv, 167, V, i, 170.

JANE

Methinks it should tear your clothes, sir.

CHOUGH

Not a rag, i'faith.—Trimtram, hold my cloak.—I'll wrestle
a fall with you now; I'll show you a trick that you never saw
in your life.   160

JANE

Oh, good sir, forbear! I am no wrestler.

PHYSICIAN

Good sir, take heed, you'll hurt the gentlewoman.

CHOUGH

I will not catch beneath the waist, believe it: I know fair play.

JANE

'Tis no woman's exercise in London, sir.

CHOUGH

I'll ne'er believe that: the hug and the lock between man and   165
woman, with a fair fall, is as sweet an exercise for the body as
you'll desire in a summer's evening.

PHYSICIAN

Sir, the gentlewoman is not well.

CHOUGH

It may be you are a physician, sir.

PHYSICIAN

'Tis so, sir.   170

CHOUGH

I say, then, and I'll stand to't, three ounces of wrestling with
two hips, a yard of a green gown put together in the inturn
is as good a medicine for the green-sickness as ever breathed.

---

165 *hug . . . lock* wrestling holds (here suggesting sexual activity)
173 *green-sickness* see 1.15 and note

---

159 *fall.* 'whosoeuer ouerthroweth his mate in such sorte, as that either his
    backe, or the one shoulder, and the contrary heele do touch the ground,
    is accounted to giue the *fall*' (Carew, loc. cit.).
163 *catch . . . waist.* A bawdy *double-entendre*, but also a genuine rule in
    Cornish wrestling: 'This hath also his lawes of taking hold onely aboue
    girdle' (ibid).
166 *fair fall.* A technical term in wrestling (cited by Fuller, loc. cit.),
    punning on *fall* = 'a woman's yielding to copulation' (Partridge, *s.v.*).
172 *green gown.* Dress stained with green through love-making in the grass.
    Cf. Herrick's poem, 'Corinna's Going a-Maying', ll.51–2.
172 *inturn.* Another wrestling term bawdily employed: 'the act of putting a
    leg between the thighs of an opponent and lifting him up' (*OED*, *sb.*,
    3).

TRIMTRAM
Come, sir, take your cloak again; I see here will be ne'er a
match.   175
JANE
[*Aside*] A match? I'd rather be matched from a musket's
mouth, and shot unto my death.
CHOUGH
I'll wrestle with any man for a good supper.
TRIMTRAM
Ay, marry, sir, I'll take your part there, catch that catch may.
PHYSICIAN
[*To* RUSSELL] Sir, she is willing to't: there at my house   180
She shall be private, and near to my attendance.
I know you'll not mistrust my faithful care;
I shall return her soon and perfectly.
RUSSELL
Take your charge, sir.—Go with this gentleman, Jane;
But prithee, look well this way ere thou go'st: 185
'Tis a rich simplicity of great estate;
A thing that will be ruled, and thou shalt rule;
Consider of your sex's general aim,
That domination is a woman's heaven.
JANE
I'll think on't, sir.
RUSSELL
                My daughter is retiring, sir.   190
CHOUGH
I will part at Dartmouth with her, sir. [*Kisses* JANE]—Oh
that thou didst but love wrestling! I would give any man three
foils on that condition.
TRIMTRAM
There's three sorts of men that would thank you for 'em,
either cutlers, fencers, or players.   195

176 *matched* fired by a slow match or fuse (not in *OED*)
179 *catch . . . may* proverbial. Cf. Tilley, C189
182 *you'll* Q2 (you Q1)   192 *give* allow (as a handicap)

---

189 *domination . . . heaven.* Proverbial; cf. Chaucer, *The Wife of Bath's
    Tale*, l.1038, and Tilley, W723.
193 *foils.* 'If [the opponent] be endangered, and make a narrow escape, it is
    called a *foyle*' (Carew, loc. cit.).
194–5 *There's . . . players.* Trimtram's feeble joke concerns *foil* = 'light-
    weight sword used in fencing'. Players used the weapons in stage-
    combats; cf. *Henry V*, IV, Prol., 50.

RUSSELL

Sir, as I began, I end—wondrous welcome!

Exit RUSSELL, JANE, PHYSICIAN, ANNE

TRIMTRAM

What, will you go to school today? You are entered, you know, and your quarterage runs on.

CHOUGH

What! to the roaring-school? Pox on't, 'tis such a damnable noise, I shall never attain it neither. I do wonder they have   200 never a wrestling-school; that were worth twenty of your fencing or dancing-schools.

TRIMTRAM

Well, you must learn to roar here in London; you'll never proceed in the reputation of gallantry else.

CHOUGH

How long has roaring been an exercise, thinkest thou,   205 Trimtram?

TRIMTRAM

Ever since guns came up: the first was your Roaring Meg.

CHOUGH

Meg? Then 'twas a woman was the first roarer?

TRIMTRAM

Ay, a fire of her touch-hole, that cost many a proper man's life since that time; and then the lions, they learnt it from the   210 guns, living so near 'em; then it was heard to the Bankside, and the bears they began to roar; then the boys got it, and so ever since there have been a company of roaring boys.

CHOUGH

And how long will it last, thinkest thou?

198 *quarterage* quarterly subscription
207 *up* to London. Cf. I, i, 416
209 *proper* handsome

---

207 *Roaring Meg.* A cannon of large bore in Edinburgh Castle. Here confused with Long Meg of Westminster, a celebrated virago of the 16th century (see H & S, X, 674).
209 *touch-hole.* The obscenity is obvious; see Partridge, pp. 121, 203.
210 *lions.* Kept in the Tower of London.
212 *bears.* In the Bankside, the area south of the Thames where several playhouses were situated, bears were baited at the Hope theatre (perhaps where the play was first acted) and at the Bear Garden and Paris Garden.

TRIMTRAM

As long as the water runs under London Bridge, or watermen   215
at Westminster Stairs.

CHOUGH

Well, I will begin to roar too, since it is in fashion. Oh
Corineus, this was not in thy time! I should have heard on't
by the tradition of mine ancestors—for I'm sure there were
Choughs in thy days—if it had been so. When Hercules and   220
thou wert on the Olympic Mount together, then was wrestling in request.

TRIMTRAM

Ay, and that mount is now the Mount in Cornwall: Corineus
brought it thither under one of his arms, they say.

CHOUGH

Oh Corineus, my predecessor, that I had but lived in those   225
days to see thee wrestle! On that condition I had died
seven year ago.

TRIMTRAM

Nay, it should have been a dozen at least, i'faith, on that
condition.   *Exeunt*

215–16 *watermen . . . Stairs*. i.e., 'forever'. The stairs (landing-place) was in
    constant use, as the quickest way to Westminster from the City was to
    be rowed there by a waterman (boatman). See Sugden, p. 561.
218 *Corineus*. One of the Trojan heroes who came to Britain with Brutus,
    the great-grandson of Aeneas, and ruled over Cornwall.
219–20 *I'm . . . days*. An ironic play on *chough* = 'simpleton'.
220–4 *When . . . say*. Corineus vanquished the giant Gogmagog in a
    wrestling-match and became the founder of the sport in Cornwall (see
    Geoffrey of Monmouth, *Historia Regum Britanniae*, I). No story exists
    of a match with Hercules or of Mt Olympus's translation to Cornwall:
    Chough and Trimtram have got their mythologies absurdly muddled.
228–9 *Nay . . . condition*. The joke seems to be that Trimtram regards
    Corineus and Hercules as near contemporaries of himself.

Act III, Scene i

Enter CAPTAIN AGER *with his two* FRIENDS

CAPTAIN AGER
　Well, your wills now?
1 CAPTAIN'S FRIEND
　　　　　　　　　Our wills? our loves, our duties
　To honoured fortitude: what wills have we
　But our desires to nobleness and merit,
　Valour's advancement, and the sacred rectitude
　Due to a valorous cause?
CAPTAIN AGER
　　　　　　　　　Oh, that's not mine!　　　　　　　5
2 CAPTAIN'S FRIEND
　War has his court of justice, that's the field,
　Where all cases of manhood are determined,
　And your case is no mean one.
CAPTAIN AGER
　　　　　　　　True; then 'twere virtuous;
　But mine is in extremes foul and unjust.
　Well, now y'ave got me hither, y'are as far　　　　10
　To seek in your desire as at first minute;
　For by the strength and honour of a vow,
　I will not lift a finger in this quarrel.
1 CAPTAIN'S FRIEND
　How? not in this? Be not so rash a sinner!
　Why, sir, do you ever hope to fight again then?　　15
　Take heed on't, you must never look for that:
　Why, the universal stock of the world's injury
　Will be too poor to find a quarrel for you.
　Give up your right and title to desert, sir:
　If you fail virtue here, she needs you not　　　　20
　All your time after; let her take this wrong,
　And never presume then to serve her more;
　Bid farewell to the integrity of arms,
　And let that honourable name of soldier

9　*in extremes* in the highest degree, extremely. An uncommon usage;
　　cf. *3 Henry VI*, III, ii, 115
17–18　echoing Ager's words at II, i, 2–3

Fall from you like a shivered wreath of laurel   25
By thunder struck from a desertless forehead,
That wears another's right by usurpation.
Good Captain, do not wilfully cast away
At one hour all the fame your life has won:
This is your native seat; here you should seek   30
Most to preserve it; or if you will dote
So much on life—poor life, which in respect
Of life in honour is but death and darkness—
That you will prove neglectful of yourself,
Which is to me too fearful to imagine,   35
Yet for that virtuous lady's cause, your mother,
Her reputation, dear to nobleness
As grace to penitence, whose fair memory
E'en crowns fame in your issue, for that blessedness
Give not this ill place, but in spite of hell,   40
And all her base fears, be exactly valiant.

CAPTAIN AGER
    Oh—oh—oh!

2 CAPTAIN'S FRIEND
            Why, well said, there's fair hope in that;
    Another such a one.

CAPTAIN AGER
            Came they in thousands,
    'Tis all against you.

1 CAPTAIN'S FRIEND
            Then, poor friendless merit,
    Heaven be good to thee! Thy professor leaves thee.   45

        Enter COLONEL *and his two* FRIENDS

He's come: do but you draw, we'll fight it for you.

26 *desertless* undeserving
30 *native seat* place where you were born, family home
31 *it* i.e., your fame
40 *Give . . . place* do not let this evil remain
41 *exactly* see II, i, 236
46 *come* ed. (comd Q1)

25–7 *like . . . usurpation.* Laurel was regarded as proof against lightning,
    provided the wearer deserved the prestige which it symbolized. Cf.
    Marvell, 'An Horatian Ode', ll.23–4.
46 *we'll . . . you.* The friend's proposal is a reasonable one, since at this
    time it was common, especially in France, for the seconds on either side
    to join in the fight.

CAPTAIN AGER
  I know too much to grant that.
1 CAPTAIN'S FRIEND
                    Oh dead manhood!
  Had ever such a cause so faint a servant?
  Shame brand me, if I do not suffer for him.
COLONEL
  I've heard, sir, y'ave been guilty of much boasting   50
  For your brave earliness at such a meeting:
  Y'ave lost the glory of that way this morning;
  I was the first today.
CAPTAIN AGER
                    So were you ever
  In my respect, sir.
1 CAPTAIN'S FRIEND [*Aside to* 2 CAPTAIN'S FRIEND]
                    Oh most base praeludium!
CAPTAIN AGER
  I never thought on victory, our mistress,   55
  With greater reverence than I have your worth,
  Nor ever loved her better.
1 CAPTAIN'S FRIEND
                    'Slight, I could knock
  His brains about his heels, methinks!
2 CAPTAIN'S FRIEND
                              Peace, prithee, peace.
CAPTAIN AGER
  Success in you has been my absolute joy,
  And when I have wished content, I have wished your friendship.   60
1 CAPTAIN'S FRIEND
  Stay, let me but run him through the tongue a little;
  There's lawyer's blood in't, you shall see foul gear straight.
2 CAPTAIN'S FRIEND
  Come, you are as mad now as he's cowardous.
COLONEL
  I came not hither, sir, for an encomium.

  54 *praeludium* prelude
  57 *'Slight* by God's light
  57–8 *'Slight . . . methinks* prose in Q1
  59 *Success in you* my successful friendship with you
  62 *gear* pus

  62 *lawyer's blood.* Lawyers were popularly noted for lubricity and dilator-
     iness.

1 CAPTAIN'S FRIEND
    No, the more coxcomb he that claws the head   65
    Of your vainglory with't!
COLONEL
                    I came provided
    For storms and tempests, and the foulest season
    That ever rage let forth, or blew in wildness
    From the incensed prison of man's blood.
CAPTAIN AGER
    'Tis otherwise with me: I come with mildness,   70
    Peace, constant amity, and calm forgiveness;
    The weather of a Christian and a friend.
1 CAPTAIN'S FRIEND
    Give me a valiant Turk, though not worth tenpence, rather.
CAPTAIN AGER
    Yet, sir, the world will judge the injury mine,
    Insufferable mine, mine beyond injury: 75
    Thousands have made a less wrong reach to hell,
    Ay, and rejoiced in his most endless vengeance—
    A miserable triumph, though a just one.
    But when I call to memory our long friendship,
    Methinks it cannot be too great a wrong   80
    That then I should not pardon. Why should man,
    For a poor hasty syllable or two,
    And vented only in forgetful fury,
    Chain all the hopes and riches of his soul
    To the revenge of that, die, lost forever?   85

---

67 *season* weather 76–8 cf. II, i, 22–3

65–6 *the more . . . with't.* He is even more of a fool to flatter your vainglory
    with it (his encomium); *coxcomb* quibbles on 'comb', and *claw* = (i)
    scratch (ii) flatter, fawn upon (*OED, v.*, 4).
73 *tenpence.* 'Turk of tenpence' was a common derogatory expression. The
    sum for some reason implied cheapness; cf. *Women Beware Women,*
    III, ii, 70.
75 *Insufferable.* Adjectives were often used adverbially; see Abbott,
    Shakespearian Grammar, sec. 1. All editors except Lamb emend.
75 *injury.* Perhaps caught from the line above (cf. the errors at IV, i, 109
    and V, i, 32). The copy may have read 'indurance', its similarity to
    Q1's 'iniury' abetting the error.
77 *his.* The antecedent could be either 'hell' (though it is spoken of as
    feminine at l.41) or 'Thousands', since such confusions of number were
    common.

For he that makes his last peace with his Maker
In anger, anger is his peace eternally:
He must expect the same return again
Whose venture is deceitful; must he not, sir?

COLONEL

I see what I must do: fairly put up again;   90
For here'll be nothing done, I perceive that.

CAPTAIN AGER

What shall be done in such a worthless business,
But to be sorry, and to be forgiven;
You, sir, to bring repentance, and I pardon?

COLONEL

I bring repentance, sir?

CAPTAIN AGER

                    If it be too much   95
To say repentance, call it what you please, sir;
Choose your own word; I know you're sorry for't,
And that's as good.

COLONEL

                    I sorry? By fame's honour, I am wronged!
Do you seek for peace, and draw the quarrel larger?

CAPTAIN AGER

Then 'tis I'm sorry that I thought you so.   100

1 CAPTAIN'S FRIEND

A captain? I could gnaw his title off!

CAPTAIN AGER

Nor is it any misbecoming virtue, sir,
In the best manliness to repent a wrong,
Which made me bold with you.

1 CAPTAIN'S FRIEND

                    I could cuff his head off.

2 CAPTAIN'S FRIEND

Nay, pish!   105

1 CAPTAIN'S FRIEND

Pox on him, I could eat his buttock baked, methinks.

90 *put up* sheathe my sword
97–8 *Choose . . . good* one line in Q1

86–7 *For . . . eternally.* A central idea of Middleton's anti-duelling pamphlet, *The Peacemaker*, which condemns those who, 'adventuring to leave
this life in anger, presume to press into the next . . . which is all
peace and love, without peace, love, or charity . . . As we have kept the
Peace, we shall be rewarded with Peace, and kept in Eternal Peace'
(Bullen, VIII, 338, 346).

COLONEL

So, once again take thou thy peaceful rest, then;

[*Puts up his sword*]

But as I put thee up, I must proclaim
This captain here, both to his friends and mine,
That only came to see fair valour righted, 110
A base submissive coward. So, I leave him. *Offers to go away*

CAPTAIN AGER

Oh, heaven has pitied my excessive patience,
And sent me a cause! Now I have a cause:
A coward I was never.—Come you back, sir!

COLONEL

How!

CAPTAIN AGER

You left a coward here?

COLONEL

Yes, sir; with you. 115

CAPTAIN AGER

'Tis such base metal, sir, 'twill not be taken;
It must home again with you.

2 CAPTAIN'S FRIEND

Should this be true now!

1 CAPTAIN'S FRIEND

Impossible: coward do more than bastard?

COLONEL

I prithee, mock me not; take heed you do not;
For if I draw once more, I shall grow terrible, 120
And rage will force me do what will grieve honour.

CAPTAIN AGER

Ha, ha, ha.

COLONEL

He smiles! Dare it be he?—What think you, gentlemen?
Your judgements, shall I not be cozened in him?
This cannot be the man. Why, he was bookish, 125
Made an invective lately against fighting—
A thing, in troth, that moved a little with me—

116 *base metal* (i) debased coin (ii) base valour
124 *cozened* deceived

125 *bookish*. Two strong indictments of duelling had been published in
1614: James I's *Edict and Severe Censure against Private Combats* and
Bacon's *Charge . . . touching Duels.*

Put up a fouler contumely far
Than thousand 'cowards' came to, and grew thankful.
CAPTAIN AGER
    Blessed remembrance in time of need!   130
    I'd lost my honour else.
2 CAPTAIN'S FRIEND
                    Do you note his joy?
CAPTAIN AGER
    I never felt a more severe necessity,
    Then came thy excellent pity.—Not yet ready?
    Have you such confidence in my just manhood,
    That you dare so long trust me, and yet tempt me   135
    Beyond the toleration of man's virtue?
    Why, would you be more cruel than your injury?
    Do you first take pride to wrong me, and then think me
    Not worth your fury? Do not use me so;
    I shall deceive you then. Sir, either draw,   140
    And that not slightingly, but with the care
    Of your best preservation, with that watchfulness
    As you'd defend yourself from circular fire,
    Your sin's rage, or her lord—this will require it—
    Or you'll be too soon lost; for I've an anger   145
    Has gathered mighty strength against you, mighty;
    Yet you shall find it honest to the last,
    Noble and fair.
COLONEL
                I'll venture't once again;
    And if't be but as true as it is wondrous,
    I shall have that I come for.—Your leave, gentlemen.   150
                        [*They draw their swords*]
1 CAPTAIN'S FRIEND
    If he should do't indeed, and deceive's all now!
    Stay, by this hand he offers—fights, i'faith;
    Fights, by this light he fights, sir!

128 *Put up* submitted to
130 *remembrance* reminder
132 *necessity* lack (of a worthy cause)
144 *her lord* sin's lord, Satan
150 *gentlemen* Q2 (Gent. Q1)

___

143 *circular fire.* Sampson's gloss, 'firing from all sides', is plausible, though
    the reference may be to the fires of hell (thus anticipating the next line).

2 CAPTAIN'S FRIEND
                                        So methinks, sir.
1 CAPTAIN'S FRIEND
    An absolute punto; hay!
2 CAPTAIN'S FRIEND
                              'Twas a passado, sir.
1 CAPTAIN'S FRIEND
    Why, let it pass, and 'twas; I'm sure 'twas somewhat.   155
    What's that now?
2 CAPTAIN'S FRIEND
                      That's a punto.
1 CAPTAIN'S FRIEND
                              Oh, go to, then;
    I knew 'twas not far off. What a world's this!
    Is coward a more stirring meat than bastard, my masters?
    Put in more eggs, for shame, when you get children,
    And make it true court-custard.—[*The* COLONEL *falls*]
                              Ho, I honour thee!   160
    'Tis right and fair, and he that breathes against it,
    He breathes against the justice of a man,
    And man to cut him off 'tis no injustice.
    Thanks, thanks, for this most unexpected nobleness!
CAPTAIN AGER
    Truth never fails her servant, sir, nor leaves him   165
    With the day's shame upon him.

154 *absolute* faultless
    punto stroke or thrust with the sword-point
    hay Italian *hai*, 'you have it', on a thrust reaching the antagonist
    passado forward thrust, one foot being advanced at the same time
155 *and* if
159 *get* beget

158–60 *Is . . . court-custard.* Sampson's interpretation seems broadly cor-
    rect: 'since a mild insult is resented when a desperate one is not, the
    next generation should be the product of mere artificial politeness'.
158 *coward.* This must refer punningly to some kind of dish, probably a
    type of custard (at this time a pie made with meat, eggs, and milk); cf.
    the jingle 'cowardy, cowardy, custard'.
158 *stirring meat.* (Sexually) stimulating food; punning on *stirring* = 'rous-
    ing to action'.
158 *bastard.* Sweet Spanish wine, taken with eggs as an aphrodisiac.
160 *court-custard.* 'Court' as an adjective implied affectation and insincer-
    ity; *OED* gives *court-cream* = 'insincere flattery'.

1 CAPTAIN'S FRIEND
                              Th'ast redeemed
    Thy worth to the same height 'twas first esteemed.
                              Exeunt CAPTAIN *and his* FRIENDS
1 COLONEL'S FRIEND
    Alas, how is it, sir? Give us some hope
    Of your stay with us; let your spirit be seen
    Above your fortune: the best fortitude   170
    Has been of fate ill-friended. Now force your empire,
    And reign above your blood, spite of dejection;
    Reduce the monarchy of your abler mind,
    Let not flesh straiten it.
COLONEL
                              Oh, just heaven has found me,
    And turned the stings of my too hasty injuries   175
    Into my own blood! I pursued my ruin,
    And urged him past the patience of an angel:
    Could man's revenge extend beyond man's life,
    This would ha' waked it. If this flame will light me
    But till I see my sister, 'tis a kind one;   180
    More I expect not from't. Noble deserver!
    Farewell, most valiant and most wronged of men;
    Do but forgive me, and I am victor then.
                              Exeunt, led by them

171 *force . . . empire* enforce your domination
172 *dejection* abasement
173 *Reduce* restore
    abler i.e., more apt to rule than the body ('blood' or 'flesh')
174 *straiten it* restrict its power
175–6 *turned . . . Into* cf. II, i, 138 and note. Punning on the sense
    'transformed'

175 *stings* ed. (strings Q1). In support of Dyce's emendation cf. Mid-
    dleton's *The Puritan*, V, iv, 51 and *A Game at Chess*, II, ii, 87: 'The
    stronger sting it shoots into the blood'.

[Act III, Scene ii]

Enter PHYSICIAN, JANE, ANNE, DUTCH NURSE *with the child*

PHYSICIAN

Sweet frow, to your most indulgent care
Take this my heart's joy. I must not tell you
The value of this jewel in my bosom.

NURSE

Dat you may vell, sir; der can niet forstoor you.

PHYSICIAN

Indeed I cannot tell you: you know, nurse,   5
These are above the quantity of price.
Where is the glory of the goodliest trees,
But in the fruit and branches? The old stock
Must decay, and sprigs, scions such as these,
Must become new stocks from us to glory   10
In their fruitful issue; so we are made
Immortal one by other.

NURSE

You spreek a most lieben fader, and ich sall do de best of
tender nurses to dis infant, my pretty frokin.

PHYSICIAN

I know you will be loving: here, sweet friend,   *Give money*   15
Here's earnest of a large sum of love and coin
To quit your tender care.

JANE

                I have some reason too
To purchase your dear care unto this infant.

                     Gives her money

---

  1 *frow* Md. Dutch *vrouw*, 'woman'
  6 *These* jewels, i.e., children
    above . . . price cannot be valued in terms of mere money
  13 *lieben* dear (German *lieb*)
  14 *frokin* little child, not necessarily female (Md. Dutch *vrouwken*)
  16 *earnest* money paid as an instalment or pledge
  17 *quit* repay

---

s.d. DUTCH. At this time the term included both High and Low German.
    4 *der . . . you*. 'There is nothing to stop you'; *forstoor* here is from Md.
    Dutch *verstoren*, 'hinder, prevent': cf. l.20 and note.
    8-11 *The . . . issue*. The metaphor is from the practice of 'striking' cut-
    tings, in which slips (scions) are taken from the parent plants (stocks)
    and set in the earth.

NURSE

You be de witness of de baptim, dat is, as you spreken, de
godimother; ich vell forstoor it so.   20

JANE

Yes, I am the bad mother—if it be offence.   *Aside*

ANNE

I must be a little kind too.   *Gives her money*

NURSE

Much tanks to you all. Dis child is much beloven, and ich
sall see much care over it.

PHYSICIAN

Farewell.—Good sister, show her the way forth.—   25
I shall often visit you, kind nurse.

NURSE

You sall be velcome.   *Exeunt* ANNE *and* NURSE

JANE

Oh sir, what a friend have I found in you!
Where my poor power shall stay in the requital,
Yourself must from your fair condition   30
Make up in mere acceptance of my will.

PHYSICIAN

Oh, pray you urge it not: we are not born
For ourselves only; self-love is a sin;
But in our loving donatives to others
Man's virtue best consists: love all begets;   35
Without, all are adulterate and counterfeit.

JANE

Your boundless love I cannot satisfy,
But with a mental memory of your virtues;

25 *Farewell . . . show* ed. (Farewell good sister: Show Q1)
34 *donatives* gifts
36 *adulterate* spurious

---

20 *forstoor*. From Md. Dutch *verstaan*, 'understand'.

28ff. The following scene is imitated closely, down to verbal particulars, in
The Changeling, III, iv, where De Flores claims the right to enjoy
Beatrice in reward for the murder of Alonzo. E. Engleberg, 'A
Middleton-Rowley Dispute', *NQ*, 198 (1953), 330–2, gives full details
of the borrowing, but concludes unjustifiably that it proves Middleton's
common authorship.

29–31 'Where my small capacity for rewarding you falls short, you must
make it up out of the kindness of your disposition merely by accepting
my (good) intentions'. Cf. Tilley, W393, 'To take the will for the deed'.

38 'Except by remembering your virtuous behaviour' (instead of rewarding it).

Yet let me not engage your cost withal:
Beseech you then take restitution   40
Of pains and bounty which you have disbursed
For your poor debtor.
PHYSICIAN
                    You will not offer it:
Do not esteem my love so mercenary
To be the hire of coin! Sure, I shall think
You do not hold so worthily of me   45
As I wish to deserve.
JANE
                    Not recompense?
Then you will beggar me with too much credit.
Is't not sufficient you preserve my name,
Which I had forfeited to shame and scorn,
Cover my vices with a veil of love,   50
Defend and keep me from a father's rage,
Whose love, yet infinite, not knowing this,
Might, knowing, turn a hate as infinite:
Sure, he would throw me ever from his blessings,
And cast his curses on me! Yes, further,   55
Your secrecy keeps me in the state of woman;
For else what husband would choose me his wife,
Knowing the honour of a bride were lost?
I cannot number half the good you do me
In the concealed retention of my sin;   60
Then make me not worse than I was before,
In my ingratitude, good sir.
PHYSICIAN
                    Again?
I shall repent my love, if you'll so call't,
To be made such a hackney. Give me coin?
I had as lieve you gave me poison, lady,   65
For I have art and antidotes 'gainst that;
I might take that, but this I will refuse.

39 *engage your cost* involve you in expense
47 *credit* punning on *credit* = 'esteem'
48 *Is't* ed. (If Q1)
56 *state of woman* reputation as a chaste (and therefore honourable)
   woman
64 *hackney* mean hireling
65 *had as lieve* would as willingly

56–8 *Your . . . lost.* The physician is not informed of Jane's betrothal.

JANE

    Will you then teach me how I may requite you
    In some small quantity?

PHYSICIAN

               'Twas that I looked for.—   *Aside*

    Yes, I will tell you, lady, a full quittance,   70
    And how you may become my creditress.

JANE

    I beseech you do, sir.

PHYSICIAN

               Indeed I will, lady:
    Not in coin, mistress, for silver, though white,
    Yet it draws black lines; it shall not rule my palm,
    There to mark forth his base corruption.   75
    Pay me again in the same quality
    That I to you tendered—that's love for love.
    Can you love me, lady? You have confessed
    My love to you.

JANE

          Most amply.

PHYSICIAN

                 Why, faith, then,
    Pay me back that way.

JANE

           How do you mean, sir?   80

PHYSICIAN

    Tush, our meanings are better understood
    Than shifted to the tongue: it brings along
    A little blabbing blood into our cheeks,
    That shames us when we speak.

JANE

             I understand you not.

PHYSICIAN

    Fie, you do; make not yourself ignorant   85
    In what you know; you have ta'en forth the lesson
    That I would read to you.

    68 *Will* ed. (Well Q1)
    70 *quittance* recompense
    73–4 *silver . . . lines* proverbial. 'White silver draws black lines'
        (Tilley, S459)
    74 *rule* (i) mark as with a ruler (ii) govern
    83 *blabbing* tell-tale. Cf. II, ii, 101
    86 *ta'en forth* learnt

JANE
                        Sure then I need not
   Read it again, sir.
PHYSICIAN
                        Yes, it makes perfect:
   You know the way unto Achilles' spear;
   If that hurt you, I have the cure, you see.   90
JANE
   Come, y'are a good man; I do perceive you,
   You put a trial to me: I thank you,
   Y'are my just confessor, and, believe me,
   I'll have no further penance for this sin.
   Convert a year unto a lasting ever,   95
   And call't Apollo's smile: 'twas once, then never.
PHYSICIAN
   Pray you mistake me not; indeed I love you.
JANE
   In deed? what deed?
PHYSICIAN
                        The deed that you have done.
JANE
   I cannot believe you.
PHYSICIAN
                        Believe the deed then.
                                   [*Offers to kiss her*]
JANE
   Away, y'are a blackamoor! You love me?   100
   I hate you for your love! Are you the man

 88 *perfect* fully conversant
100 *blackamoor* used of any dark-skinned person. A common term of
    abuse

 89 *Achilles' spear*. Telephus, wounded with Achilles' spear, was cured with
    its rust; see Ovid, *Metamorphoses*, XII, 112, XIII, 171–2. Rowley has
    the unlettered man's fondness for parading his knowledge without
    regard for aptness; cf. Shakespeare's use of the image in *2 Henry VI*,
    V, i, 100. The main point seems to be the phallic quibble.
95–6 'Let a year last for all eternity, and then call that a mere instant: in
    all that time I shall never commit this sin again'. *Apollo's smile* is
    obscure, but is apparently meant to suggest the briefness of a sunbeam.
 98 *In deed*. All editors follow Q1's 'Indeed'; cf. *Antony and Cleopatra*, I, v,
    16 where Jaggard's Compositor B suppressed the same pun by the
    reverse error.

That in your painted outside seemed so white?
Oh, y'are a foul dissembling hypocrite!
You saved me from a thief that yourself might rob me,
Skinned o'er a green wound to breed an ulcer: 105
Is this the practice of your physic-college?

PHYSICIAN

Have you yet uttered all your niceness forth?
If you have more, vent it; certes I think
Your first grant was not yielded with less pain;
If 'twere, you have your price, yield it again.   110

JANE

Pray you tell me, sir—I asked it before—
Is it a practice 'mongst you physicians?

PHYSICIAN

Tush, that's a secret; we cast all waters.
Should I reveal, you would mistrust my counsel:
The lawyer and physician here agrees,   115
To women clients they give back their fees;
And is not that kindness?

JANE

                        This for thy love!   *Spits*
Out, outside of a man: thou cinnamon-tree,
That but thy bark hast nothing good about thee!
The unicorn is hunted for his horn,   120

102 *painted* specious
    white unstained, virtuous
105 *green* fresh, unhealed
107 *niceness* coyness
108 *certes* assuredly
109 *grant* consent (to love-making)

---

105 *Skinned o'er*. Cf. *Hamlet*, III, iv, 147: 'It will but skin and film the ulcerous place'.
106 *physic-college*. The Royal College of Physicians, founded in 1518 by Thomas Linacre.
113 *we . . . waters*. 'We have an eye to every opportunity (for profit)'. Combining a reference to uroscopy, the art of divining a patient's malady from his urine, with the proverbial tag, 'I am for all waters'; cf. *Twelfth Night*, IV, ii, 61.
118–19 *thou . . . thee*. A commonplace; cf. Overbury, *Characters*, 'A Fine Gentleman': he is 'the Cynamon tree, whose barke is more worth then his body'.
120 *horn*. Powdered unicorn's horn was thought an antidote against poison. The physician's value, like that of the unicorn and the cinnamon-tree, lies only in his ability to heal; otherwise he is worthless.

The rest is left for carrion. Thou false man,
Th'ast fished with silver hooks and golden baits;
But I'll avoid all thy deceiving sleights.
PHYSICIAN
Do what you list, I will do something too.
Remember yet what I have done for you: 125
Y'ave a good face now, but 'twill grow rugged;
Ere you grow old, old men will despise you.
Think on your grandam Helen, the fairest queen:
When in a new glass she spied her old face,
She, smiling, wept to think upon the change.   130
Take your time: y'are crazed, y'are an apple fall'n
From the tree; if you be kept long, you'll rot.
Study your answer well: yet I love you;
If you refuse, I have a hand above you.   *Exit* PHYSICIAN
JANE
Poison thyself, thou foul empoisoner;   135
Of thine own practic drink the theory!
What, a white devil have I met withal?
What shall I do?—What do? Is't a question?
Nor shame, nor hate, nor fear, nor lust, nor force,

---

123 *sleights* wiles
128 *grandam* ancestress. *OED* cites no such usage before 1620 (*sb.*, 2)
131 *Take your time* seize your opportunity
     crazed cracked (in reputation)
134 *above you* ed. (om. you Q1)

---

122 *fished . . . baits.* 'Ventured more than you stood to gain'. Proverbial,
     though here not particularly appropriate; see Tilley, H591.
128–30 *Think . . . change.* Dyce notes that the incident is recounted in
     Metamorphoses, XV, 232–6, and dramatized in the final scene of
     Heywood's *2 The Iron Age* (acted *c.* 1612).
130 *smiling.* Presumably as she poses before the mirror.
131–2 *apple . . . tree.* A stock metaphor for a ruined maid; cf. *All's Lost by
     Lust*, II, i, 84–6.
136 *Of . . . theory.* i.e., do to yourself as you do to others; *practic* puns on
     (i) practice (in contradistinction to theory) (ii) cunning.
137 *white devil.* Devil disguised under a fair outside (referring back to
     ll.100–3). Cf. Tilley, D310: 'The white devil is worse than the black'.

Now being too bad, shall ever make me worse.   140

Enter ANNE

What have we here? a second spirit?
ANNE
                                        Mistress,
I am sent to you.
JANE
                        Is your message good?
ANNE
As you receive it: my brother sent me,
And you know he loves you.
JANE
                                I heard say so;
But 'twas a false report.   145
ANNE
Pray pardon me, I must do my message;
Who lives commanded must obey his keeper.
I must persuade you to this act of woman.
JANE
Woman? of strumpet!
ANNE
                        Indeed, of strumpet.
He takes you at advantage of your fall,   150
Seeing you down before.
JANE
                        Curse on his feigned smiles!
ANNE
He's my brother, mistress; and a curse on you,
If e'er you bless him with that cursed deed.
Hang him, poison him! He held out a rose

---

141 *spirit* i.e., evil spirit which draws man into sin
150 *fall* see II, ii, 166 and note

141ff. Sampson explains the contradictoriness of Anne's advice by suggesting that the physician is eavesdropping: 'Anne speaks aloud in his
favour, but gives her honest opinions *sotto voce*'. Q1's lack of direction
makes it safer to assume, however, that Anne is acting as Jane's
self-appointed moral tester. Either way the aim is to expound her
dilemma and demonstrate her unshakeable honesty.

To draw the yielding sense, which, come to hand, 155
He shifts, and gives a canker.

JANE

You speak well yet.

ANNE

Ay, but mistress, now I consider it,
Your reputation lies at his mercy,
Your fault dwells in his breast; say he throw it out,
It will be known; how are you then undone! 160
Think on't, your good name; and they are not to be sold
In every market: a good name's dear,
And indeed more esteemed than our actions,
By which we should deserve it.

JANE

Ay me, most wretched!

ANNE

What! do you shrink at that? 165
Would you not wear one spot upon your face
To keep your whole body from a leprosy,
Though it were undiscovered ever? Hang him,
Fear him not. Horse-leeches suck out his corrupt blood;
Draw you none from him, 'less it be pure and good. 170

JANE

Do you speak your soul?

ANNE

By my soul do I.

JANE

Then yet I have a friend: but thus exhort me,
And I have still a column to support me.

ANNE

One fault heaven soon forgives, and 'tis on earth forgot;
The moon herself is not without one spot. *Exeunt* 175

155 *draw* entice   156 *shifts* changes (transitive)
161–2 *they . . . market* cf. the proverb 'Love is not found in the
market' (Tilley, L511)
162 *dear* (i) expensive (ii) precious
166 *spot* see II, ii, 76 and note

156 *canker*. The dog- or wild rose, regarded as inferior to the garden rose.
    The point, as in Shakespeare's Sonnet LIV, is that while it is like the
    garden rose to look at, the canker has no smell.
169 *Horse-leeches*. Larger than the common medicinal leech, and (wrongly)
    considered voracious feeders.
175 *The . . . spot*. Proverbial; see Tilley, S782, V31. In medieval cosmo-
    graphy only the sublunary world contained imperfection.

[Act III, Scene iii]

Enter the LADY AGER, *meeting one of her* SERVANTS

LADY AGER
  Now, sir, where is he? Speak, why comes he not?
  I sent you for him.—Bless this fellow's senses!
  What has he seen? A soul nine hours entranced,
  Hovering 'twixt hell and heaven, could not wake ghastlier.

Enter SERVANT

  Not yet return an answer?—What say you, sir?   5
  Where is he?
2 SERVANT
        Gone!
LADY AGER
           What say'st thou?
2 SERVANT
                      He is gone, madam;
  But, as we heard, unwillingly he went
  As ever blood enforced.
LADY AGER
           Went? Whither went he?
2 SERVANT
  Madam, I fear I ha' said too much already.
LADY AGER
  These men are both agreed.—Speak, whither went he?   10
2 SERVANT
  Why, to—I would you'd think the rest yourself, madam.
LADY AGER
  Meek patience bless me!
2 SERVANT
           To the field.
1 SERVANT
                To fight, madam.
LADY AGER
  To fight!
1 SERVANT
  There came two urging gentlemen,

8 *enforced* better taken as a past participle
10 *agreed* united (in a conspiracy). See *OED*, *ppl.a.*, 3, 4

---

3 *nine*. Three times three, and hence a mystic number (Sampson); cf. IV,
ii, 48–9.

That called themselves his seconds; both so powerful,
As 'tis reported, they prevailed with him   15
With little labour.

LADY AGER
                              Oh, he's lost, he's gone!
For all my pains, he's gone! Two meeting torrents
Are not so merciless as their two rages:
He never comes again.—Wretched affection!
Have I belied my faith? injured my goodness?   20
Slandered my honour for his preservation,
Having but only him, and yet no happier?
'Tis then a judgement plain: truth's angry with me,
In that I would abuse her sacred whiteness
For any worldly temporal respect.   25
Forgive me then, thou glorious woman's virtue,
Admired where'er thy habitation is,
Especially in us weak ones; oh, forgive me,
For 'tis thy vengeance this. To belie truth,
Which is so hardly ours, with such pain purchased,   30
Fastings and prayers, continence and care,
Misery must needs ensue. Let him not die
In that unchaste belief of his false birth
And my disgrace; whatever angel guides him,
May this request be with my tears obtained,   35
Let his soul know my honour is unstained.—
Run, seek, away! If there be any hope,   *Exeunt* SERVANTS
Let me not lose him yet. When I think on him,

19 *affection* love
23 *truth* see II, i, 101 and note
24 *whiteness* purity
26 *thou . . . virtue* chastity
28–9 *me, . . . this.* ed. (me. . . . this, Q1)
30 *Which . . . ours* which we attain with so much difficulty

---

15–16 *they . . . labour.* This is false (cf. II, i, 214ff.) and contradicts the
    second servant's account at l.7. The discrepancy is intentional, since
    Lady Ager now speaks her soliloquy believing that her desperate
    expedient has proved utterly futile.
20 *belied.* Not until this point are the spectators certain of Lady Ager's
    innocence, save by the art of the performer (Sampson).
33 *false birth.* Sampson comments 'This was not a necessary inference',
    but see II, i, 183 and note.

His dearness and his worth, it earns me more:
They that know riches tremble to be poor.   40
My passion is not every woman's sorrow:
She must be truly honest feels my grief,
And only known to one; if such there be,
They know the sorrow that oppresseth me.   *Exit*

Act IV, Scene i

Enter the COLONEL'S FRIEND, USHER, *etc.* [*i.e.*, ROARERS,] *with*
CHOUGH *and* TRIMTRAM

COLONEL'S FRIEND
Truth, sir, I must needs blame you for a truant, having but
one lesson read to you, and neglect so soon; fie, I must see
you once a day at least.

CHOUGH
Would I were whipped, tutor, if it were not long of my man
Trimtram here.   5

TRIMTRAM
Who, of me?

CHOUGH
[*Aside to* TRIMTRAM] Take't upon thee, Trim; I'll give thee
five shillings, as I am a gentleman.

TRIMTRAM
[*Aside to* CHOUGH] I'll see you whipped first!—Well, I will

---

39 *it . . . more* I am the more afflicted by grief (see *OED*, 'earns',
    v.³, 2)
40 *They . . . poor* proverbial. Cf. Tilley, M1098, R108–9
41 *passion* (i) suffering (ii) passionate feeling
s.d. FRIEND ed. (*Second* Q1)
    USHER assistant schoolmaster
 1 s.p. COLONEL'S FRIEND ed. (throughout this scene Q1 abbreviates
    for *Second*)
 4 *long of* on account of (aphetic form of 'along of')

---

39 *dearness . . . worth . . . earns*. Punning on the pecuniary senses; cf. I, i,
    17 and III, ii, 162.
43 *known to one*. Known sexually to only one man. Cf. *More Dissemblers*,
    II, i, 81: 'she's part virgin who but one man knows'.
s.d. ROARERS. Often depicted as in a contemporary ballad, *The Cheating
    Age*, with 'long shaggy locks', 'long rustie Rapiers, swolne eyes, &
    patcht faces' (in *A Pepysian Garland*, ed. H. E. Rollins, 1922).

too.—Faith, sir, I saw he was not perfect, and I was loth he   10
should come before to shame himself.

COLONEL'S FRIEND

How! shame, sir? Is it a shame for scholars to learn? Sir,
there are great scholars that are but slenderly read in our
profession. Sir, first it must be economical, then ecumenical:
shame not to practise in the house how to perform in the field.   15
The nail that is driven takes a little hold at the first stroke,
but more at the second, and more at the third, but when 'tis
home to the head, then 'tis firm.

CHOUGH

Faith, I have been driving it home to the head this two days.

TRIMTRAM

I helped to hammer it in as well as I could too, sir.   20

COLONEL'S FRIEND

Well, sir, I will hear you rehearse anon; meantime peruse the
exemplary of my bills, and tell me in what language I shall
roar a lecture to you; or I'll read to you the mathematical
science of roaring.

CHOUGH

Is it mathematical?   25

COLONEL'S FRIEND

Oh sir, does not the winds roar? the sea roar? the welkin roar?
Indeed, most things do roar by nature, and is not the knowledge of these things mathematical?

CHOUGH

Pray proceed, sir.

COLONEL'S FRIEND

Reads his bill The names of the languages, the Sclavonian,   30

---

10 *perfect* fully conversant, as at ll.34, 145
14 *economical* domestic, restricted to the household
   then Q1 corrected (the Q1 uncorrected)
   ecumenical universal
16–18 *nail . . . firm* cf. the proverb 'Drive the nail to the head'
   (Tilley, N15)
22 *exemplary* copy
   bills handbills (for advertising purposes)
26 *does* see I, i, 404 and note
   welkin heaven, sky. Often used in phrases describing loud
   sounds
28 *mathematical* quibbling on the sense 'astrological' (*OED, a.*, 3)
30 *Sclavonian* Slavonian

Parthamenian, Barmeothian, Tyburnian, Wappinganian, or
the modern Londonian: any man or woman that is desirous
to roar in any of these languages, in a week they shall be
perfect if they will take pains; so let 'em repair into Holborn
to the sign of the Cheat Loaf.   35

CHOUGH
Now your bill speaks of that I was wondering a good while at,
your sign: the loaf looks very like bread, i'faith, but why is
it called the Cheat Loaf?

COLONEL'S FRIEND
This house was sometimes a baker's, sir, that served the
court, where the bread is called cheat.   40

TRIMTRAM
Ay, ay, 'twas a baker that cheated the court with bread.

COLONEL'S FRIEND
Well, sir, choose your languages; and your lectures shall be
read, between my usher and myself, for your better instruction, provided your conditions be performed in the premises
beforesaid.   45

CHOUGH
Look you, sir, there's twenty pound in hand, and twenty
more I am to pay when I am allowed a sufficient roarer.

COLONEL'S FRIEND
You speak in good earnest, sir?

---

36 *that . . . at*, ed. (that, . . . at Q1)
39 *sometimes* formerly
47 *sufficient* qualified

---

31 *Parthamenian.* Rowley probably conflated 'Parthian' and 'Armenian'.
31 *Barmeothian.* From *Barmoothes*, a common form of *Bermudas*, the name
   of a notorious quarter of London near Covent Garden. See
   Introduction, p. xviii.
31 *Tyburnian.* Criminals were hanged at Tyburn.
31 *Wappinganian.* Wapping, on the north bank of the Thames below
   London docks, was the place where pirates were hanged.
32 *or woman.* Perhaps in deference to Moll Cutpurse, the real-life epony-
   mous heroine of Middleton and Dekker's *The Roaring Girl.* Cf. II, ii, 208.
40 *court . . . cheat.* Although coarser than manchet, cheat bread was 'vsed
   in the houses of the nobilitie, and gentry onely' (W. Harrison, *An
   Historical Description of the Island of Britain*, 1577, f. 95ᵛ).
41 *baker . . . bread.* The malpractices of the royal bakers were a standing
   joke; cf. *Your Five Gallants*, III, ii, 98–9: 'chipped away like a court
   loaf, that . . . has nothing but bumbast'.

CHOUGH

Yes, faith, do I; Trimtram shall be my witness.

TRIMTRAM

Yes indeed, sir, twenty pound is very good earnest.   50

USHER

Sir, one thing I must tell you belongs to my place: you are the youngest scholar, and till another comes under you, there is a certain garnish belongs to the school; for in our practice we grow to a quarrel, then there must be wine ready to make all friends—for that's the end of roaring, 'tis valiant,   55
but harmless—and this charge is yours.

CHOUGH

With all my heart, i'faith, and I like it the better because no blood comes on it. Who shall fetch?

ROARER

I'll be your spaniel, sir.

COLONEL'S FRIEND

Bid Vapour bring some tobacco too.   60

CHOUGH

Do, and here's money for't.

USHER

No, you shall not; let me see the money.—*Exit* ROARER
So, I'll keep it, and discharge him after the combat. For your practice sake you and your man shall roar him out on't—for indeed you must pay your debts so, for that's one of the main   65
ends of roaring—and when you have left him in a chafe, then I'll qualify the rascal.

50 *earnest* quibbling on the sense at III, ii, 16
56 *charge* either 'duty' or 'expense' could be meant
59 s.p. ROARER ed. (here and at ll.62, 113 s.d. Q1 designates for 2. *Roarer*)
66 *chafe* rage
67 *qualify* pacify

53 *garnish*. Illegal fee, here in a specialized slang sense: 'money extorted from a new prisoner as drink-money for the other prisoners' (*OED*, *sb.*, 5).
59 *I'll . . . sir*. A familiar expression: 'Yes, sir, I'm your Water-spaniell, and will fetch anything' (Dekker, *2 The Honest Whore*, IV, iii, 30).
60 *tobacco*. Roarers were regularly associated with the newly fashionable habit of smoking (or 'drinking') tobacco; cf. *The Alchemist*, III, iv, 22–3.

CHOUGH

Content, i'faith.—Trim, we'll roar the rusty rascal out of
his tobacco.

TRIMTRAM

Ay, and he had the best crocus in London.   70

COLONEL'S FRIEND

Observe, sir, we could now roar in the Sclavonian language,
but this practice hath been a little sublime, some hair's
breadth or so above your caput; I take it, for your use and
understanding both, it were fitter for you to taste the modern
assault, only the Londonian roar.   75

CHOUGH

I'faith, sir, that's for my purpose, for I shall use all my
roaring here in London: in Cornwall we are all for wrestling,
and I do not mean to travel over sea to roar there.

COLONEL'S FRIEND

Observe then, sir:—but it were necessary you took forth your
tables, to note the most difficult points for the better   80
assistance of your memory.

CHOUGH

Nay, sir, my man and I keep two tables.

TRIMTRAM

Ay, sir, and as many trenchers, cats' meat and dogs' meat
enough.

COLONEL'S FRIEND

Note, sir.—Dost thou confront my cyclops?   85

---

68 *Content . . . Trim,* ed. (Content ifaith *Trim.* Q1)
   rusty churlish
70 *and* (even) if
78 *over sea* Chough's geography reflects his provincialism
80 *tables* memorandum-books
83 *trenchers* wooden serving-plates

---

70 *crocus* ed. (Craccus Q1). A type of tobacco. Not in *OED*, though the
   word occurs in this sense in Fletcher's *The Woman's Prize*, I, ii, p. 6:
   'Selling (which is a sin unpardonable) . . . musty English *Croacus*'. The
   origin is clearly Latin *crocus*, 'saffron', since *saffron-cut* was also a kind
   of tobacco. All editors follow Q1, and *craccus* even appears in *OED*, but
   none furnishes a second example.
73 *caput.* A quite preposterous quibble on (i) head (ii) residue left after
   'sublimation' (the conversion of solids into vapour).
82 *keep . . . tables.* Eat at separate tables. Rowley prolongs the agony by
   having Trimtram understand 'own two tables'.
85ff. The slanging-match had a long history in the drama stretching back
   to the Morality plays. On a general level the 'quarrel' mocks the

USHER
With a Briarean brousted.
CHOUGH
[*Writes*] Cyclops.
TRIMTRAM
[*Writes*] Briarean.
COLONEL'S FRIEND
I know thee and thy lineal pedigree.
USHER
It is collateral, as Brutus and Posthumus.   90
TRIMTRAM
Brutus.
CHOUGH
Posthumus.
COLONEL'S FRIEND
False as the face of Hecate! Thy sister is a—
USHER
What is my sister, centaur?
COLONEL'S FRIEND
I say thy sister is a bronstrops.   95
USHER
A bronstrops!
CHOUGH
Tutor, tutor, ere you go any further, tell me the English of
that; what is a bronstrops, pray?

---

employment of eccentric private languages by sections of the Jacobean
underworld (see Dekker's *Lanthorn and Candlelight*, 1609, ch. I, 'Of
Canting'), but Rowley is also sending up a particular aspect of the
roarers' notoriety, their taste for flamboyant oaths; cf. the roaring boy
in *The Cheating Age*: 'This tatterd grim Rascall amaz'd me to heare,/
The terrible oathes which for nothing he sware'.

86 *Briarean brousted*. Baffling. *Briareus* was the hundred-handed giant who
fought against Zeus, but *brousted* defies analysis.

89 *I . . . pedigree*. A turgid equivalent of 'son of a whore'. Lineal descent is
descent in a direct line.

90 *collateral*. Descent from the same stock but in a different line. Posthumus, however, was the grandson and thus the lineal descendant of
Brutus.

93 *Hecate*. Goddess of the underworld, but traditionally identified with
Diana, goddess of the moon; cf. Tilley, M1111: 'As changeful as the
moon'.

95 *bronstrops*. A compound of the names *Brontes* and *Steropes*, two of the
cyclops, which Rowley probably found in John Weever's *Epigrams*,
1599. See Margery Fisher, 'Bronstrops. A Note on *A Faire Quarrell*',
MLR, 35 (1940), 59–62.

COLONEL'S FRIEND
A bronstrops is in English a hippocrene.
CHOUGH
A hippocrene; note it, Trim; I love to understand the   100
English as I go.
TRIMTRAM
What's the English of hippicrene?
CHOUGH
Why, bronstrops!
USHER
Thou dost obtrect my flesh and blood.
COLONEL'S FRIEND
Again I denounce, thy sister is a fructifer.   105
CHOUGH
What's that, tutor?
COLONEL'S FRIEND
That is in English a fucus or a minotaur.
CHOUGH
[*Writes*] A minotaur.
TRIMTRAM
[*Writes*] A fucus.
USHER
I say thy mother is a calicut, a panagron, a duplar, and a   110
sindicus.

104 *obtrect* disparage
105 *fructifer* from 'fructify', with an obvious quibble
107 *fucus* a type of cosmetic. The pun is elaborated at IV, iv, 59
109 s.p. TRIMTRAM ed. (*Chau.* Q1 *Sec.* Q2)
110 *panagron* Greek for 'fishing-net'
    duplar meaningless, presumably glancing at *dupe*, 'to cheat'
111 *sindicus* Latin for 'advocate'

99 *hippocrene*. A fountain on Mt Helicon sacred to the Muses. Incon-
   gruous among the other classical names which, as names of monsters,
   can with comparative rationality be used to mean 'whore'. Perhaps
   confused with *hippogryph*.
102 *hippicrene*. All editors normalize to *hippocrene*, but Q1's spelling may
    represent mispronunciation.
107 *minotaur*. Perhaps chosen because the Cretan monster fed on human
    flesh.
110 *calicut*. The early form of *Calcutta*, with a double sexual quibble: on
    callet, 'whore', and on *cut* (cf. *A Chaste Maid*, II, i, 35: 'Can any
    woman have a greater cut?').

COLONEL'S FRIEND

[*Draws his sword*] Dislocate thy blade!

USHER

Bladud shall conjure, if his demons once appear.

Enter ROARER *with wine, and* VAPOUR *with tobacco*

COLONEL'S FRIEND

Advance thy respondency!

CHOUGH

Nay, good gentlemen, do not fall out.—A cup of wine quickly, 115
Trimtram!

USHER

[*Draws his sword*] See, my steel hath a glister!

CHOUGH

Pray wipe him, and put him up again, good usher.

USHER

Sir, at your request I pull down the flag of defiance.

COLONEL'S FRIEND

Give me a bowl of wine, my fury shall be quenched.—Here, 120
usher!   [*Drinks*]

USHER

I pledge thee in good friendship.   [*Drinks*]

CHOUGH

I like the conclusion of roaring very well, i'faith.

TRIMTRAM

It has an excellent conclusion indeed, if the wine be good,
always provided.   125

COLONEL'S FRIEND

Oh, the wine must be always provided, be sure of that.

USHER

Else you spoil the conclusion, and that you know crowns all.

112 *Dislocate* remove, draw
114 *Advance . . . respondency* periphrastically, perhaps either 'reci-
procate' (i.e., draw your sword) or 'on guard'
115 *gentlemen* ed. (gentleman Q1)
118 *Pray . . . again* punning obscenely on *glister* = 'suppository'
127 *conclusion . . . all* proverbial. 'The end crowns all' (Tilley, E116)

112 *blade*. All editors retain Q1's *Bladud*, which was evidently caught from
the following line (note the similar error only three lines before).
113 *Bladud*. A legendary British king who was 'addicted . . . to the deuilish
arte of Necromancie' (T. Beard, *The Theatre of God's Judgement*, 1597,
sig. I1ᵛ).

CHOUGH

'Tis much like wrestling, i'faith, for we shake hands ere we
begin; now that's to avoid the law, for then if he throw him
a furlong into the ground, he cannot recover himself upon   130
him, because 'twas done in cold friendship.

COLONEL'S FRIEND

I believe you, sir.

CHOUGH

And then we drink afterwards, just in this fashion: wrestling
and roaring are as like as can be, i'faith, even like long sword
and half-pike.   135

COLONEL'S FRIEND

Nay, they are reciprocal, if you mark it, for as there is a great
roaring at wrestling, so there is a kind of wrestling and
contention at roaring.

CHOUGH

True, i'faith, for I have heard 'em roar from the six windmills
to Islington; those have been great falls then.   140

COLONEL'S FRIEND

Come, now a brief rehearsal of your other day's lesson,
betwixt your man and you, and then for today we break up
school.

CHOUGH

Come, Trimtram.—If I be out, tutor, I'll be bold to look in
my tables, because I doubt I am scarce perfect.   145

COLONEL'S FRIEND

Well, well, I will not see small faults.

CHOUGH

The wall!

129 *he . . . him* the wrestler and his opponent
130 *recover . . . upon* obtain legal judgement against   145 *doubt* fear

---

134–5 *long sword . . . half-pike.* Not 'as like as can be' either in appearance
or as matched in combat: the 'halfe Pike . . . or such like weapons of
perfect length, haue the vantage against . . . the two hand sword' (G.
Silver, *Paradoxes of Defence*, 1599, p. 31). Possibly the comparison
merely demonstrates Chough's ignorance, but a similar coupling of the
terms in *The Old Law*, III, ii, 175–84, suggests that an ulterior
meaning, probably bawdy, awaits elucidation. Both *pike* and *sword*
could mean 'penis' (see Partridge, *s.v.*).

139 *windmills.* In Finsbury Fields, east of Islington (Sugden, p. 568).
Wrestling matches were held there.

147 *wall.* As the cleanest part of the pavement was usually that farthest
from the street, taking the wall from inferiors was regarded as a point
of honour; cf. *Romeo and Juliet*, I, i, 12.

TRIMTRAM
  The wall of me? to thy kennel, spaniel!
CHOUGH
  Wilt thou not yield precedency?
TRIMTRAM
  To thee? I know thee and thy brood.   150
CHOUGH
  Know'st thou my brood? I know thy brood too: thou art a
  rook.
TRIMTRAM
  The nearer akin to the choughs!
CHOUGH
  The rooks akin to the choughs?
COLONEL'S FRIEND
  Very well maintained.   155
CHOUGH
  Dungcart, thou liest!
TRIMTRAM
  Lie? enucleate the kernel of thy scabbard!
CHOUGH
  Now, if I durst draw my sword, 'twere valiant, i'faith.
COLONEL'S FRIEND
  Draw, draw, howsoever.
CHOUGH
  Have some wine ready to make us friends, I pray you.   160
TRIMTRAM
  Chough, I will make thee fly and roar.
CHOUGH
  I will roar if thou strik'st me.
COLONEL'S FRIEND
  So, 'tis enough; now conclude in wine. I see you will prove
  an excellent practitioner: wondrous well performed on both
  sides!   165

---

148 *kennel* punning on *kennel* = 'gutter'
     spaniel commonly used of a fawning flatterer
152 *rook* gull, fool. Trimtram counters by playing on the regular sense
157 *enucleate* extract. Cf. 1.112
161 *fly* (i) fly (ii) flee

---

156 *Dungcart* ed. (Dungcoer Q1). A term of opprobrium; cf. Heywood, *The
     Captives*, in A. H. Bullen, ed., *Old English Plays*, 4 vols., 1882–85, IV,
     111: 'thou father of fornication ... thou dungcart of diseases'. All
     editors retain Q1's nonsensical reading without comment.

CHOUGH

Here, Trimtram, I drink to thee.   [*Drinks*]

TRIMTRAM

I'll pledge you in good friendship.   [*Drinks*]

Enter a SERVANT

[SERVANT]

Is there not one Master Chough here?

USHER

This is the gentleman, sir.

SERVANT

My master, sir, your elected father-in-law, desires speedily   170
to speak with you.

CHOUGH

Friend, I will follow thee. I would thou hadst come a little
sooner; thou shouldst have seen roaring sport, i'faith.

SERVANT

Sir, I'll return that you are following.

CHOUGH

Do so.—   *Exit* SERVANT   175
I'll tell thee, tutor, I am to marry shortly, but I will defer
it a while till I can roar perfectly, that I may get the upper
hand of my wife on the wedding-day; 'tmust be done at first
or never.

COLONEL'S FRIEND

'Twill serve you to good use in that, sir.   180

CHOUGH

How lik'st thou this, whiffler?

VAPOUR

Very valiantly, i'faith, sir.

CHOUGH

Tush, thou shalt see more by and by.

VAPOUR

I can stay no longer indeed, sir. Who pays me for my tobacco?

---

167 *you* Q1 corrected (om. Q1 uncorrected)

---

181 *whiffler*. Smoker of tobacco. Rowley's coinage from 'whiff', a puff of
tobacco-smoke, and 'whiffler', the steward who cleared the way at the
head of a procession, sometimes blowing a pipe or horn.

183ff. A flurry of anti-smoking pamphlets appeared in the early 17th
century, James I himself contributing *A Counterblast to Tobacco*, 1604.
Besides the topical appeal of the subject, the prospect of the play's
court performance may thus have prompted the lengthy diatribe which
follows.

CHOUGH

How! pay for tobacco? Away, ye sooty-mouthed piper! you　185
rusty piece of Martlemas bacon, away!

TRIMTRAM

Let me give him a mark for't.

CHOUGH

No, Trimtram, do not strike him; we'll only roar out a curse
upon him.

TRIMTRAM

Well, do you begin then.　　　　　　　　　　　　　190

CHOUGH

May thy roll rot, and thy pudding drop in pieces, being
sophisticated with filthy urine!

TRIMTRAM

May sergeants dwell on either side of thee, to fright away thy
twopenny customers!

CHOUGH

And for thy penny ones, let them suck thee dry!　　　　195

TRIMTRAM

When thou art dead, mayst thou have no other sheets to be
buried in but mouldy tobacco-leaves!

CHOUGH

And no strawings to stick thy carcass but the bitter stalks!

---

185 *piper* pipe-smoker. *OED* cites no such usage before 1632
186 *rusty* rancid. 'Bacon . . . yf you hang it in great smoke . . . it wyl
be rustie' (B. Googe, *Four Books of Husbandry*, 1577, f. 152ᵛ)
187 *mark* money to the value of 13sh. 4d. The pun is common
191 *roll* tobacco-leaves rolled together into a cylindrical shape
pudding tobacco in a compressed form
196 *sheets* winding-sheets
198 *strawings* flowers scattered on a corpse or grave

---

185 *sooty-mouthed.* 'Smoke . . . makes a kitchin also oftentimes in the in-
ward parts of men, soiling and infecting them, with an vnctuous and
oily kinde of Soote' (James I, op. cit., sig. D1ʳ).
186 *Martlemas bacon.* Bacon salted on St Martin's Day, 11 November.
Rowley is making a familiar comparison; J. Deacon describes an
autopsy on some smokers whose 'very fat in their bodies' resembled
'the perfect colour of rustie, or reesed bacon' (*Tobacco Tortured*, 1616,
sig. A1ʳ).
192 *sophisticated . . . urine.* The complaint was common; cf. *Bartholomew
Fair*, II, vi, 26 and *The Alchemist*, I, iii, 27.
198 *stick.* Cf. *Romeo and Juliet*, IV, v, 79–80: 'Dry up your tears, and stick
your rosemary/On this fair corse'.

TRIMTRAM
   Thy mourners all greasy tapsters!
CHOUGH
   With foul tobacco-pipes in their hats instead of rotten rose-   200
   mary! And last of all, may my man and I live to see all this
   performed, and to piss reeking even upon thy grave!
TRIMTRAM
   And last of all for me, let this epitaph be remembered over
   thee:

   Here coldly now within is laid to rot   205
   A man that yesterday was piping hot:
   Some say he died by pudding, some by prick,
   Others by roll and ball, some leaf; all stick
   Fast in censure, yet think it strange and rare,
   He lived by smoke, yet died for want of air: 210
   But then the surgeon said, when he beheld him,
   It was the burning of his PIPE *that killed him.*

CHOUGH
   So, are you paid now, whiffler?
VAPOUR
   All this is but smoke out of a stinking pipe.
CHOUGH
   So, so, pay him now, usher.   215
COLONEL'S FRIEND
   Do not henceforth neglect your schooling, Master Chough.
CHOUGH
   Call me rook if I do, tutor.
TRIMTRAM
   And me raven, though my name be Trimtram.
CHOUGH
   Farewell, tutor.

199 *tapsters* drawers of beer in a tavern
206 *piping* quibbling on the sense 'smoking tobacco'
207 *prick* small roll of tobacco, with a sexual pun
208 *ball . . . leaf* types of tobacco (with a pun on 'ball')
209 *censure* opinion
210 *air* punning on 'hair' (which falls out in the final stages of syphilis)

---

200 *hats.* It was fashionable as well as convenient to keep one's pipes in
   one's hat-band.
200–1 *rosemary.* The plant was worn at weddings and funerals as a symbol
   of remembrance. See note to l.198.
202 *piss . . . grave.* In reply to the malpractice denounced at l.192.
212 *burning.* The pun concerns *burn* = 'to infect with venereal disease', and
   the bawdy sense of *pipe* (see Partridge, *s.v.*).

TRIMTRAM
    Farewell, usher.   [*Exeunt* CHOUGH *and* TRIMTRAM]   220
COLONEL'S FRIEND
    Thus, when the drum's unbraced, and trumpet cease,
    Soldiers must get pay for to live in peace.   *Exeunt*

[Act IV, Scene ii]

[*The* COLONEL *discovered lying in a bed, his two* FRIENDS
attending him.] *Enter the* COLONEL'S SISTER, *meeting the*
                    SURGEON

COLONEL'S SISTER
    Oh my most worthy brother, thy hard fate 'twas!—
    Come hither, honest surgeon, and deal faithfully
    With a distressed virgin: what hope is there?
SURGEON
    Hope? chilis was 'scaped miraculously, lady.
COLONEL'S SISTER
    What's that, sir?   5
SURGEON
    Cava vena. I care but little for his wound i'th' oesophag, not

---

6 *Cava vena* the *venae cavae* are the two main veins returning the
   blood to the heart
   oesophag ed. (*Orso-/phag* Q1) obsolete form of 'oesophagus'

---

221 *trumpet.* Emended to 'trumpets' by other editors, but occasionally
    found in a plural sense; cf. *Henry V*, III, ii, 103.
s.d. Q1's inadequate direction obscures the staging of this scene. The
    gravity of the Colonel's wounds suggests that he should appear in bed,
    but he and his friends could be suitably discovered at l.39, since the
    sister's opening remark may be merely a snatch of soliloquy designed to
    identify her to the audience. (As evidence of compositorial omission
    one could point out that l.39 begins a new sheet in Q1.) However, as
    the Colonel's immediate discovery explains the presence of the surgeon,
    and gives an underlying poignancy to his comical diagnosis, I follow
    previous editors.
s.d. SURGEON. Regarded as a craftsman, and the social inferior of the
    physician, an intellectual.
  4ff. Middleton's voluble and wordy surgeon represents a standard joke
    against the medical profession, which was often criticized for using
    technical jargon merely to impress patients; cf. Sweetball, the barber-
    surgeon of Middleton's *Anything for a Quiet Life.*
  4 *chilis.* 'Out of the gibbosyte or bounch of the liuer, there issueth a
    veyne called concaua or chillis' (J. Vigo, *The Most Excellent Works of
    Chirurgery*, 1543, f.ix[r]).

thus much [*snaps his fingers*], trust me; but when they come to
diaphragma once, the small intestines, or the spinal medul,
or i'th' roots of the emunctories of the noble parts, then
straight I fear a syncope; the flanks retiring towards the back,   10
the urine bloody, the excrements purulent, and the dolour
pricking or pungent.

COLONEL'S SISTER
Alas, I'm ne'er the better for this answer!

SURGEON
Now I must tell you his principal dolour lies i'th' region of
the liver, and there's both inflammation and tumefaction   15
feared: marry, I made him a quadrangular plumation, where
I used sanguis draconis, by my faith, with powders incarnative, which I tempered with oil of hypericon, and other
liquors mundificative.

COLONEL'S SISTER
Pox o' your mundies figatives! I would they were all fired!   20

SURGEON
But I purpose, lady, to make another experiment at next

---

 7 *they* i.e., wounds
 8 *diaphragma* diaphragm, midriff
   medul marrow
 9 *emunctories* excretory ducts and organs
   noble parts those parts of the body without which life cannot be
   maintained
10 *syncope* ed. (*Syncops* Q1) heart-failure
11 *dolour* pain
12 *pricking* causing sharp pain
   pungent = 'pricking'
15 *tumefaction* ed. (*Turma-/faction* Q1) swelling
16 *quadrangular* ed. (*Quadragular* Q1)
17–18 *incarnative* promoting the growth of flesh in a wound
19 *liquors mundificative* detergent solutions
20 *fired* burned

---

16 *plumation*. 'Plumations are made of little peeces of cloth . . . wooll, or
   towe, the pith of Elder tree, the haires of a Hare, Gentian'; their
   purpose, to 'conserue the substance and the temperature of the hurt
   part, and consolide the wound' (Lowe, *Discourse of the Whole Art of
   Chirurgery*, p. 295).
17 *sanguis draconis*. A red palm-gum; 'astringent . . . it closeth up wounds'
   (J. Woodall, *The Surgeon's Mate*, 1617, edn. 1639, p. 74).
18 *oil of hypericon*. Prepared from the plant St John's wort; 'healing
   sinewes pricked or wounded . . . good to cure new wounds' (ibid., p.
   48).

dressing with a sarcotic medicament made of iris of Florence:
thus, mastic, calaphena, opoponax, sacrocolla—
COLONEL'S SISTER
Sacro-halter! What comfort is i' this to a poor gentlewoman?
Pray tell me in plain terms what you think of him.   25
SURGEON
Marry, in plain terms I know not what to say to him: the
wound, I can assure you, inclines to paralism, and I find his
body cacochymic; being then in fear of fever and inflamma-
tion, I nourish him altogether with viands refrigerative, and
give for potion the juice of sanicula dissolved with water   30
cerefolium: I could do no more, lady, if his best ginglymus
were dissevered.   *Exit*
COLONEL'S SISTER
What thankless pains does the tongue often take
To make the whole man most ridiculous!
I come to him for comfort, and he tires me   35
Worse than my sorrow. What a precious good
May be delivered sweetly in few words,
And what a mount of nothing has he cast forth!—

22 *sarcotic* ed. (*Sarcotricke* Q1) = 'incarnative'
28 *cacochymic* having unhealthy or unbalanced 'humours'
29 *viands refrigerative* victuals which cool the body
31 *ginglymus* ed. (*Guiguimos* Q1) hinge-like joint, allowing motion in
   two directions

---

22 *iris of Florence.* Florentine or white iris, from which orris-root, a
   common vulnerary, is obtained.
23 *mastic.* An eastern gum; 'It helpeth concoction, stoppeth vomiting'
   (Woodall, op. cit., p. 72).
23 *calaphena.* 'Colophonia . . . is a kind of Rosin of the Pine tree . . . hot
   and drie, cleansing and healing new wounds' (ibid., p. 7).
23 *opoponax.* Another gum-resin; 'it doth mollifie, digest, attenuate or
   assuage . . . and is laxative' (ibid., p. 71).
23 *sacrocolla.* Sarcocolla, a red medicinal gum from Persia. The erroneous
   form, which conveniently makes way for the sister's retort, was trans-
   ferred by Middleton from Lowe, *Discourse*, p. 280.
27 *paralism.* Lowe's slip (ibid.), copied by Middleton, for *paralisie*, paralysis.
30 *sanicula* ed. (*Sauicola* Q1). Sanicle, a plant. 'The iuice being inwardly
   taken is good to heale wounds' (J. Gerard, *The Herbal*, 1597, p. 802).
   All editors retain Q1's meaningless corruption.
31 *cerefolium.* Chervil, a herb, which Lowe (p. 321) prescribes for a patient
   who, like the Colonel, has a wound in the diaphragm.
33–4 *What . . . ridiculous.* Proverbial; cf. 'the tongue may undo the whole
   body' (*A Shoemaker*, I, ii, 159), and Tilley, T408.

[*Aside*] Alas, his strength decays.—How cheer you, sir,
My honoured brother?

COLONEL

In soul, never better: 40
I feel an excellent health there, such a stoutness
My invisible enemy flies me; seeing me armed
With penitence and forgiveness, they fall backward,
Whether through admiration, not imagining
There were such armoury in a soldier's soul   45
As pardon and repentance, or through power
Of ghostly valour. But I have been lord
Of a more happy conquest in nine hours now
Than in nine years before.—Oh kind lieutenants,
This is the only war we should provide for!   50
Where he that forgives largest, and sighs strongest,
Is a tried soldier, a true man in deed,
And wins the best field, makes his own heart bleed.
Read the last part of that will, sir.

                                            1 COLONEL'S FRIEND *reads*
[1 COLONEL'S FRIEND]

I also require at the hands of my most beloved sister, whom I   55
make full executrix, the disposure of my body in burial at
St. Martin's i'th' Field; and to cause to be distributed to
the poor of the same parish forty mark, and to the hospital of
maimed soldiers a hundred; lastly, I give and bequeath to my
kind, dear, and virtuous sister the full possession of my   60
present estate in riches, whether it be in lands, leases, money,
goods, plate, jewels, or what kind soever, upon this condition
following, that she forthwith tender both herself and all these

---

44 *admiration* wonder
47 *ghostly* spiritual
54 s.d 1 COLONEL'S FRIEND ed. (1 *Liefetenant* Q1)
58 *mark* see IV, i, 187

42–3 *enemy flies . . . they.* All editors emend to 'enemies fly', but this
   collective usage is still current. Cf. *Julius Caesar*, V, i, 13–14.
57 *St. Martin's.* A fashionable upper-class cemetery. See Sugden, p. 334.
57–8 *to . . . mark.* A traditional provision; cf. Shakespeare's will: 'I gyve
   and bequeath vnto the Poore of Stratford aforesaied tenn pounds'.
62–5 *upon . . . Ager.* Improbable as this type of condition now appears, at
   the time it was 'considered reasonable and enforceable under . . . common law' (Clarkson and Warren, op. cit., p. 278). Middleton repeated
   the motif from *A Woman Killed with Kindness*, but cf. the similar
   blackmailing stipulation in *The Phoenix*, I, vi, 140–1.

infeoffments to that noble captain, my late enemy, Captain
Ager.   65

COLONEL'S SISTER
How, sir?
COLONEL
Read it again, sir; let her hear it plain.
COLONEL'S SISTER
Pray spare your pains, sir; 'tis too plain already.—
Good sir, how do you? Is your memory perfect?
This will makes question of you. I bestowed   70
So much grief and compassion o' your wound,
I never looked into your sense's epilepsy:
The sickness and infirmity of your judgement
Is to be doubted now more than your body's.
Why, is your love no dearer to me, sir,   75
Than to dispose me so upon the man
Whose fury is your body's present torment,
The author of your danger, one I hate
Beyond the bounds of malice? Do you not feel
His wrath upon you? I beseech you, sir,   80
Alter that cruel article.
COLONEL
                Cruel, sister?—
Forgive me, natural love; I must offend thee,
Speaking to this woman.—Am I content,
Having much kindred, yet to give thee all,
Because in thee I'd raise my means to goodness,   85
And canst thou prove so thankless to my bounty,
To grudge my soul her peace? Is my intent
To leave her rich, whose only desire is
To send me poorer into the next world
Than ever usurer went, or politic statist?   90
Is it so burdensome for thee to love
Where I forgive? Oh, wretched is the man

64 *infeoffments* deeds of ownership (*OED*, *sb.*, 1.b)
74 *doubted* feared
81 *article* see I, i, 259
81–3 *Cruel . . . content* lineation ed.
90 *politic statist* scheming politician

69–70 *Is . . . you.* Carrying a legal implication, since a person of unsound
    mind could not make a valid will; cf. Webster, *The Devil's Law-Case*,
    II, i, 121–2: 'He died in perfect memory I hope,/And made me his
    heyre'.

That builds the last hopes of his saving comforts
Upon a woman's charity! He's most miserable:
If it were possible, her obstinate will   95
Will pull him down in his midway to heaven.
I've wronged that worthy man past recompense,
And in my anger robbed him of fair fame;
And thou the fairest restitution art
My life could yield him: if I knew a fairer,   100
I'd set thee by and thy unwilling goodness,
And never make my sacred peace of thee;
But there's the cruelty of a fate debarred:
Thou art the last, and all, and thou art hard!

COLONEL'S SISTER
Let your grieved heart hold better thoughts of me: 105
I will not prove so, sir; but since you enforce it
With such a strength of passion, I'll perform
What by your will you have enjoined me to,
Though the world never show me joy again.

COLONEL
Oh, this may be fair cunning for the time,   110
To put me off, knowing I hold not long;
And when I look to have my joys accomplished,
I shall find no such things: that were vild cozenage,
And not to be repented.

COLONEL'S SISTER
                    By all the blessedness
Truth and a good life looks for, I will do't, sir.   115

COLONEL
Comforts reward you for't, whene'er you grieve!
I know if you dare swear, I may believe.   *Exeunt*

[Act IV, Scene iii]

Enter CAPTAIN AGER

CAPTAIN AGER
No sooner have I entrance i' this house now
But all my joy falls from me, which was wont
To be the sanctuary of my comforts:
Methought I loved it with a reverend gladness,
As holy men do consecrated temples,   5

106–7 *it . . . passion, . . . perform* ed. (it, . . . passion . . . perform, Q1)
113 *vild cozenage* base trickery
  3 *sanctuary* (i) shelter (ii) holy place which grants this

For the saint's sake, which I believed my mother;
But proved a false faith since, a fearful heresy.
Oh, who'd erect th' assurance of his joys
Upon a woman's goodness, whose best virtue
Is to commit unseen, and highest secrecy   10
To hide but her own sin? There's their perfection.
And if she be so good, which many fail of too,
When these are bad, how wondrous ill are they!
What comfort is't to fight, win this day's fame,
When all my after-days are lamps of shame?   15

Enter LADY AGER

[LADY AGER]
    [*Aside*] Blessings be firm to me! He's come, 'tis he!—
    A surgeon speedily!
CAPTAIN AGER
                    A surgeon? why, madam?
LADY AGER
    Perhaps you'll say 'tis but a little wound;
    Good to prevent a danger.—Quick, a surgeon!
CAPTAIN AGER
    Why, madam?   20
LADY AGER
    Ay, ay, that's all the fault of valiant men;
    They'll not be known o' their hurts till they're past help,
    And then too late they wish for't.
CAPTAIN AGER
                            Will you hear me?
LADY AGER
    'Tis no disparagement to confess a wound;
    I'm glad, sir, 'tis no worse.—A surgeon, quickly!   25
CAPTAIN AGER
    Madam—
LADY AGER
            Come, come, sir, a wound's honourable,
    And never shames the wearer.
CAPTAIN AGER
                        By the justice
    I owe to honour, I came off untouched.
LADY AGER
    I'd rather believe that.

15 *lamps* models, paragons (intentionally paradoxical)
19 *prevent* forestall, as at 1.34

CAPTAIN AGER
                    You believe truth so.

LADY AGER
  My tears prevail then. Welcome, welcome, sir,   30
  As peace and mercy to one new departed!
  Why would you go though, and deceive me so,
  When my abundant love took all the course
  That might be to prevent it? I did that
  For my affection's sake—goodness forgive me for't—   35
  That were my own life's safety put upon't,
  I'd rather die than do't. Think how you used me then;
  And yet would you go, and hazard yourself too;
  'Twas but unkindly done.

CAPTAIN AGER
                    What's all this, madam?

LADY AGER
  See then how rash you were, and short in wisdom: 40
  Why, wrong my faith I did, slandered my constancy,
  Belied my truth; that which few mothers will,
  Or fewer can, I did, out of true fear
  And loving care, only to keep thee here.

CAPTAIN AGER
  I doubt I am too quick of apprehension now,   45
  And that's a general fault when we hear joyfully,
  With the desire of longing for't. I ask it:
  Why, were you never false?

LADY AGER
                    May death come to me
  Before repentance then!

CAPTAIN AGER
                    I heard it plain, sure—
  Not false at all?

LADY AGER
                    By the reward of truth,   50
  I never knew that deed that claims the name on't.

CAPTAIN AGER
  May then that glorious reward you swore by
  Be never-failing to you! All the blessings

35 *affection* love
39 *unkindly* contrary to the ties of kindred
42 *truth* see II, i, 101 and note
45 *doubt* fear
51 lineation ed. (That claimes . . . on't Q1 as separate line)

38 *yourself*. i.e., your soul; see II, i, 18, 151 and notes.

That you have given me, since obedient custom
Taught me to kneel and ask 'em, are not valuable   55
With this immaculate blessing of your truth:
This is the palm to victory,
The crown for all deserts past and to come:
Let 'em be numberless! They are rewarded,
Already they're rewarded. [*Kneeling*] Bless this frame,   60
I feel it much too weak to bear the joy on't.

LADY AGER
Rise, sir.

CAPTAIN AGER
Oh, pardon me—
I cannot honour you too much, too long:
I kneel not only to a mother now,   65
But to a woman that was never false.
Ye're dear, and ye're good too—ay, think o' that:
What reverence does she merit! 'Tis fit such
Should be distinguished from the prostrate sex;
And what distinction properer can be shown   70
Than honour done to her that keeps her own?

LADY AGER
Come, sir, I'll have you rise.

CAPTAIN AGER
                              To do a deed, then,   *Rises*
That shall forever raise me.—Oh my glory,
Why, this, this is the quarrel that I looked for!
The tother but a shift to hold time play.   75
You sacred ministers of preservation,
For heaven's sake send him life,
And with it mighty health, and such a strength

55–6 *are . . . With* cannot be compared in value with
75 *but . . . play* merely an expedient to occupy the time

---

56 *immaculate.* Note the religious reference here and in the next two lines.
    The imagery is realized visually at l.60.
67 *ay, think.* Other editors understand Q1's 'I thinke' as first person
    pronoun plus verb, but *ay* is regularly spelled 'I' in Q1 and often lacks
    a following comma. The imperative stresses the speaker's sense of
    wonder and anticipates his reference to Lady Ager in the third person.
71 *honour.* Perhaps here in the sense of 'bow, curtsey, obeisance', an
    uncommon meaning comparatively frequent in Middleton; see C.
    Barber, 'A Rare Use of the Word *Honour* as a Criterion of Middleton's
    Authorship', *ES*, 38 (1957), 162. Barber admits, however, a play here on
    two more familiar senses: (i) mark of esteem conferred on somebody
    (ii) female honour, chastity (since *her own* = 'her own honour').

May equal but the cause! I wish no foul things:
If life but glow in him, he shall know instantly   80
That I'm resolved to call him to accompt for't.

LADY AGER

Why, hark you, sir—

CAPTAIN AGER

               I bind you by your honour, madam,
You speak no hindrance to's; take heed, you ought not.

LADY AGER

What an unhappiness have I in goodness!
'Tis ever my desire to intend well,   85
But have no fortunate way in't. For all this
Deserve I yet no better of you
But to be grieved again? Are you not well
With honest gain of fame, with safety purchased?
Will you needs tempt a ruin that avoids you?   *Exit* LADY   90

CAPTAIN AGER

No, y'ave prevailed: things of this nature sprung,
When they use action, must use little tongue.—

Enter a SERVANT

Now, sir, the news?

SERVANT

              Sir, there's a gentlewoman
Desires some conference with you.

CAPTAIN AGER

                How! with me?
A gentlewoman? what is she?

SERVANT

              Her attendant   95
Delivered her to be the Colonel's sister.   [*Exit* SERVANT]

---

83 lineation ed. (Take . . . not Q1 as separate line)
84 *unhappiness* ill fortune
87–90 lineation ed.
89 *fame* (honourable) reputation
92 s.d. *Enter a* SERVANT ed. (follows l.93, 'Now . . . newes', in Q1)

---

91 *y'ave.* The antecedent of *you* appears to be Lady Ager, yet it is clear
from the rest of the couplet that Ager is announcing his intention to
pursue his quarrel with the Colonel. The only way to make sense of
this (short of emending to 'y'ave not') is to assume that by 'you' Ager
is referring to his mother's honour.
92 *action.* With a pun on the sense 'rhetorical gesture as an accompaniment to speech', as in the proverb 'Actions speak louder than words'.

CAPTAIN AGER
  Oh for a storm then!
  'Las, poor virtuous gentlewoman,
  I will endure her violence with much pity;
  She comes to ease her heart, good, noble soul;   100
  'Tis e'en a charity to release the burden:
  Were not that remedy ordained for women,
  Their hearts would never hold three years together.
  And here she comes—I never marked so much of her:

       Enter the COLONEL'S SISTER

  That face can be the mistress of no anger   105
  But I might very well endure a month, methinks.—
  I am the man; speak, lady; I'll stand fair.
COLONEL'S SISTER
  And I'm enjoined by vow to fall thus low,   *She kneels*
  And from the dying hand of a repentant
  Offer for expiation of wrongs done you   110
  Myself, and with myself all that was his,
  Which upon that condition was made mine,
  Being his soul's wish to depart absolute man,
  In life a soldier, death a Christian.
CAPTAIN AGER
  Oh, heaven has touched him nobly: how it shames   115
  My virtue's slow perfection! Rise, dear brightness—
  I forget manners too—up, matchless sweetness!
COLONEL'S SISTER
  I must not, sir; there is not in my vow
  That liberty. I must be received first,
  Or all denied; if either, I am free.   120
CAPTAIN AGER
  He must be without soul should deny thee;
  And with that reverence I receive the gift
  As it was sent me [*Raises her*]. Worthy Colonel,
  H'as such a conquering way i'th' blessed things!
  Whoever overcomes, he only wins.   *Exeunt* 125

---

107 *I'll . . . fair* i.e., I'll take it   113 *absolute* absolved from sin
116 *perfection* i.e., growth to perfection   125 s.d. *Exeunt* ed. (*Exit* Q1)

---

125 *Whoever . . . wins.* Ambiguous, but the most appropriate sense is
    'Whichever of us won the duel, the only real winner is the Colonel'.

[Act IV, Scene iv]

Hem, within.
Enter CAPTAIN ALBO, [MEG,] *a bawd, and* [PRISS,] *a whore*

MEG
Hark off these hard-hearted bloodhounds! These butchers
are e'en as merciless as their dogs: they knock down a
woman's fame e'en as it walks the streets by 'em.

PRISS
And the Captain here, that should defend us, walks by like
John of the apple-loft.   5

CAPTAIN ALBO
What for interjections, Priss? *Hem, evax, vah*! Let the
carnifexes scour their throats! Thou knowest there is a curse
hangs over their bloody heads: this year there shall be more
butchers' pricks burnt than of all trades besides.

MEG
I do wonder how thou camest to be a captain.   10

CAPTAIN ALBO
As thou camest to be a bawd, Meg, and Priss to be a whore;
every one by their deserts.

---

3 *fame* see IV, iii, 89
6 *What for* what do . . . matter
   Hem, evax Latin exclamations of surprise and joy
   vah Latin equivalent of English 'Oh!'
7 *carnifexes* butchers (medieval Latin). Originally 'executioners'
   curse i.e., syphilis
9 *pricks* meat-skewers, with a bawdy pun *burnt* see note to IV, i, 212
12 *every . . . deserts* proverbial. See Tilley, D207

---

s.d. *Hem.* Interjection made by a loud clearing of the throat, used by
      prostitutes or their customers as a sound of invitation.
s.d. CAPTAIN ALBO. Pimps often masqueraded as soldiers; cf. 'Captains'
      Whit and Pistol of *Bartholomew Fair* and *2 Henry IV*.
1 *Hark off.* A hunting term, 'to draw hounds off from the quarry' (*OED*,
   v., 4.a). All editors retain Q1's *of*, presumably understanding 'listen to'.
   Such a usage is without authority, whereas 'off' is regularly spelled 'of' in
   Q1.
2 *dogs.* 'Butcher dog' (*canis laniarus*) was a name for the mastiff. References to butchers by both sets of characters (see 1.44) suggest that the
   setting is Smithfield Market.
5 *John . . . apple-loft.* Obscure. Perhaps equivalent to *apple-squire*, 'pimp',
   since *apple-john* (a kind of apple eaten when shrivelled) seems to have
   this sense in *Bartholomew Fair*, I, iii, 55. An aspersion of impotence
   would better explain the comparison, however.

MEG

Bawd and whore? out, you unprofitable rascal! Hast not thou
been at the new play yet, to teach thee better manners? Truly
they say they are the finest players, and good speakers of   15
gentlewomen of our quality: 'bawd' and 'whore' is not
mentioned amongst 'em, but the handsomest narrow-
mouthed names they have for us, that some of them may
serve as well for a lady as for one of our occupation.

PRISS

Prithee, patroness, let's go see a piece of that play; if we   20
shall have good words for our money, 'tis as much as we can
deserve, i'faith.

MEG

I doubt 'tis too late now; but another time, servant.

CAPTAIN ALBO

Let's go now, sweet face; I am acquainted with one of the
pantomimics; the bulchins will use the Irish captain with   25
respect, and you two shall be boxed amongst the better sort.

PRISS

Sirrah Captain Albo, I doubt you are but white-livered:
look that you defend us valiantly, you know your penance
else.—Patroness, you remember how you used him once?

MEG

Ay, servant, and I shall never forget it till I use him so   30
again.—Do you remember, Captain?

CAPTAIN ALBO

Mum, Meg; I will not hear on't now.

MEG

How I and my Amazons stripped you as naked as an Indian—

CAPTAIN ALBO

Why, Meg!

14 *new play* i.e., this play   23 *doubt* fear
25 *pantomimics* literally 'pantomimists', here inflatedly for 'actors'.
   OED's earliest instance
   bulchins bull-calves, a term of contempt. *OED*'s earliest instance
27 *Sirrah* term of address to men or boys expressing contempt or
   assuming authority
   doubt suspect

17–18 *narrow-mouthed*. *OED* explains by quoting its earliest example
   (1667): 'Those [languages] that . . . require but very slight Motions of
   the Lips and other Organs of speech'. Meg, however, seems to mean
   'abstruse', or 'exotic', or perhaps 'elaborately polite'.
26 *boxed . . . sort*. i.e., placed in one of the 'private rooms', admission to
   which cost sixpence or a shilling (see Chambers, II, 533).

MEG

And then how I bound you to the good behaviour in the open   35
fields.

PRISS

And then you strowed oats upon his hoppers—

CAPTAIN ALBO

Prithee, sweet face!

PRISS

And then brought your ducks to nibble upon him.—You
remember?   40

CAPTAIN ALBO

Oh, the remembrance tortures me again! No more, good
sweet face.

MEG

Well, lead on, sir;—but hark a little.

Enter CHOUGH *and* TRIMTRAM

CHOUGH

Didst thou bargain for the bladders with the butcher, Trim?

TRIMTRAM

Ay, sir, I have 'em here. I'll practise to swim too, sir, and   45
then I may roar with the water at London Bridge: he that
roars by land and by water both is the perfect roarer.

CHOUGH

Well, I'll venture to swim too: if my father-in-law gives me
a good dowry with his daughter, I shall hold up my head well
enough.   50

TRIMTRAM

Peace, sir; here's practice for our roaring: here's a centaur
and two hippocrenes.

CHOUGH

Offer the justle, Trim.   *Justle*

CAPTAIN ALBO

Ha! what meanest thou by that?

TRIMTRAM

I mean to confront thee, cyclops.   55

47 *the perfect* Q2 (the the perfect Q1)

37 *hoppers.* (i) seed-baskets (ii) buttocks (not in *OED*, but cf. *hopperarsed*,
'large-buttocked', in J. O. Halliwell-Phillipps, *A Dictionary of Archaic
and Provincial Words*, 5th edn., 1901).

44 *bladders.* Used by children as water-wings; cf. *Henry VIII*, III, ii, 60.

46 *roar . . . Bridge.* The roaring of the water, due to the bridge-piers
which impeded the stream, is often commented on; cf. *Eastward Ho!*,
IV, i, 13.

CHOUGH
   I'll tell thee what 'a means—is this thy sister?
CAPTAIN ALBO
   How then, sir?
CHOUGH
   Why then, I say she is a bronstrops; and this is a fucus.
PRISS
   No indeed, sir; we are both fucusses.
CAPTAIN ALBO
   Art thou military? art thou a soldier?   60
CHOUGH
   A soldier? no, I scorn to be so poor; I am a roarer.
CAPTAIN ALBO
   A roarer?
TRIMTRAM
   Ay, sir, two roarers.
CAPTAIN ALBO
   Know then, my freshwater friends, that I am a captain.
CHOUGH
   What, and have but two to serve under you?   65
CAPTAIN ALBO
   I am now retiring the field.
TRIMTRAM
   You may see that by his bag and baggage.
CHOUGH
   Deliver up thy panagron to me.
TRIMTRAM
   And give me thy sindicus.
CAPTAIN ALBO
   Deliver?   70
MEG
   I pray you, Captain, be contented; the gentlemen seem to give
   us very good words.
CHOUGH
   Good words? ay, if you could understand 'em; the words
   cost twenty pound.
MEG
   What is your pleasure, gentlemen?   75
CHOUGH
   I would enucleate my fructifer.

64 *freshwater* callow, raw (often applied sneeringly to recruits and
   unseasoned soldiers)
65 *serve under you* with a bawdy *double entendre*
76 *enucleate* see IV, i, 157. Chough is garbling his roaring lesson

PRISS

What says he, patroness?

MEG

He would inoculate: I understand the gentleman very
pithily.

CAPTAIN ALBO

Speak, are you gentle or plebeian? Can you give arms?   80

CHOUGH

Arms? ay, sir, you shall feel our arms presently.

TRIMTRAM

'Sault you the women, I'll pepper him till he stinks again.
I perceive what countryman he is; let me alone with him.

CAPTAIN ALBO

Dar'st thou charge a captain?

TRIMTRAM

Yes, and discharge upon him too.   85

CAPTAIN ALBO

Foh, 'tis poison to my country; the slave has eaten pippins!
Oh, shoot no more, turn both thy broadsides rather than thy
poop! 'Tis foul play: my country breeds no poison. I yield;
the great O'Toole shall yield on these conditions.

CHOUGH

I have given one of 'em a fair fall, Trim.   90

78 *inoculate* at this time meaning 'to join or unite by insertion'
79 *pithily* thoroughly
80 *Can . . . arms* have you a coat of arms, are you of good family
82 *'Sault* assault, punning on 'salt'
88 *poop* stern, with a broad pun
   foul (i) unfair (ii) disgusting
90 *fair fall* see II, ii, 166 and note

82 *pepper*. Playing on (i) sprinkle with pepper (ii) give pungency or flavour
   to (iii) pelt with shot or missiles (iv) infect with venereal disease. Cf.
   the similar quibble in *The Family of Love*, V, i, 90.
86 *pippins*. Albo apparently finds the attack the more treacherous because
   pippins, a variety of apple, were traditionally a favourite Irish dish; cf.
   Rowley's pamphlet, *A Search for Money*, in *Percy Society Reprints*, II,
   1840, p. 32: 'cates to please five several nations . . . a pippin pye for
   your Irishman'.
88 *my . . . poison*. A commonplace, originating in St Patrick's ridding
   Ireland of all venomous creatures.
89 *O'Toole*. Arthur Severus O'Toole, an Irish captain 'notorious for his
   romantic bravery, vanity, and eccentricity' (Dyce), satirized by John
   Taylor in *The Great O'Toole*, 1622. Albo himself caricatures O'Toole,
   who had recently come to live in London.

TRIMTRAM

Then thus far we bring home conquest.—Follow me,
Captain; the cyclops doth command.

CHOUGH

Follow me, tweaks; the centaur doth command.

MEG

Anything, sweet gentlemen. Will't please you to lead to the
tavern, where we'll make all friends?   95

TRIMTRAM

Why, now you come to the conclusion.

CHOUGH

Stay, Trim; I have heard your tweaks are like your mermaids,
they have sweet voices to entice the passengers: let's have
a song, and then we'll set 'em at liberty.

TRIMTRAM

In the commendation of roaring—not else, sir.   100

CHOUGH

Ay, in the commendation of roaring.

MEG

The best we can, gentlemen.   *Sing bawd*

    Then here thou shalt resign
    Both captain and commander;
    That name was never thine,   105
    But apple-squire and pander;
    And henceforth will we grant,
    In pillage or in monies,
    In clothing or provant,
    Whate'er we get by conies.   110
      With a hone, a hone, a hone,
      No cheaters nor decoys
      Shall have a share, but alone
      The bravest roaring boys.

    Whate'er we get by gulls,   115
    Of country or of city,

97 *mermaids* slang for 'whores'. Cf. *All's Lost by Lust*, III, iii, 132
98 *passengers* punning on the original meaning, 'passers-by'
106 *apple-squire* pimp   109 *provant* provisions
110 *conies* fools, gulls

---

93 *tweaks*. Another roaring term for 'whores', not used in IV, i. Rowley's
coinage was adopted by several later writers (see *OED*).
111 *a hone*. A common ballad refrain; cf. *Bartholomew Fair*, V, iv, 276.
Specially appropriate here, since originally an Irish keening cry.

> *Old flatcaps or young heirs,*
> *Or lawyers' clerks so witty;*
> *By sailors newly landed,*
> *To put in for fresh waters;*   120
> *By wand'ring gander-mooners,*
> *Or muffled late night-walkers.*
>   *With a, etc.*
>
> *Whate'er we get by strangers,*
> *The Scotch, the Dutch, or Irish,*   125
> *Or to come nearer home,*
> *By masters of the parish,*
> *It is concluded thus,*
> *By all and every wench,*
> *To take of all their coins,*   130
> *And pay 'em back in French.*
>   *With a, etc.*

CHOUGH
Melodious minotaur!
TRIMTRAM
Harmonious hippocrene!
CHOUGH
Sweet-breasted bronstrops!   135
TRIMTRAM
Most tunable tweak!
CHOUGH
Delicious duplar!
TRIMTRAM
Putrefactious panagron!
CHOUGH
Calumnious calicut!

117 *flatcaps* derisory name for London citizens, from their headgear
120 *put in* with a sexual pun
    waters punning on *water* = 'semen', as at II, ii, 137
122 *muffled* wrapped up, cloaked
    night-walkers thieves, bullies
136 *tunable* tuneful
138 *Putrefactious* putrid

---

121 *gander-mooners.* Rowley's coinage from *gander-month:* 'That month in
    which a man's wife lies in: wherefore, during that time, husbands plead
    a sort of indulgence in matters of gallantry' (F. Grose, *A Classical
    Dictionary of the Vulgar Tongue*, 3rd edn., 1796).
131 *French.* i.e., French coins, and punning on 'French disease' (*morbus
    gallicus*), syphilis.

TRIMTRAM
And most singular sindicus!   140
MEG
We shall never be able to deserve these good words at your
hands, gentlemen.
CAPTAIN ALBO
Shake golls with the captain, he shall be thy valiant friend.
CHOUGH
Not yet, Captain; we must make an end of our roaring first.
TRIMTRAM
We'll serve 'em as we did the tobacco-man, lay a curse upon   145
'em; marry, we'll lay it on gently, because they have used
us so kindly; and then we'll shake golls together.
PRISS
As gently as you can, sweet gentlemen.
CHOUGH
For thee, oh pander, mayst thou trudge till the damned
soles of thy boots fleet into dirt, but never rise into air!   150
TRIMTRAM
Next, mayst thou fleet so long from place to place, till thou
beest kicked out of Fleet Street!
CHOUGH
As thou hast lived by bad flesh, so rotten mutton be thy
bane!
TRIMTRAM
When thou art dead, may twenty whores follow thee, that   155
thou mayst go a squire to thy grave!
CAPTAIN ALBO
Enough for me, sweet faces, let me sleep in my grave.
CHOUGH
For thee, old sindicus, may I see thee ride in a caroche with
two wheels, and drawn with one horse!

143 *golls* cant term for 'hands'
150 *soles* punning on 'souls'
    fleet waste away, decay (*OED*, *v.*, 9.a)
151 *fleet* drift (*OED*, *v.*, 2)
156 *a squire* with the ceremony befitting a squire. Punning on (*apple-*)
    squire = 'pimp'
158 *caroche* city coach or carriage

---

153 *bad flesh . . . rotten mutton.* Slang expressions for women, especially
    whores, infected with venereal disease. See Partridge, pp. 107, 151.
158–9 *with . . . horse.* i.e., not a real caroche, but a cart in which criminals
    were drawn through the streets. Rowley's delight in obscenity encour-
    ages suspicion of a phallic innuendo.

TRIMTRAM
> Ten beadles running by, instead of footmen!   160

CHOUGH
> With every one a whip, 'stead of an Irish dart!

TRIMTRAM
> Forty barbers' basins sounding before, instead of trumpets!

MEG
> This will be comely indeed, sweet gentlemen roarers.

TRIMTRAM
> Thy ruff starched yellow with rotten eggs!

CHOUGH
> And mayst thou then be drawn from Holborn to Hounslow   165
> Heath!

TRIMTRAM
> And then be burnt to Colebrook, for destroying of Maiden-
> head!

MEG
> I will study to deserve this kindness at your hands, gentle-
> men.   170

CHOUGH
> Now for thee, little fucus: mayst thou first serve out thy time
> as a tweak, and then become a bronstrops, as she is!

---

160 *by* alongside

---

160 *beadles.* Charged with whipping petty offenders, such as bawds and prostitutes.

161 *Irish dart.* Irishmen were commonly employed as running footmen, and it was probably fashionable to equip them with something resembling the traditional Irish weapon; cf. Dekker, *2 The Honest Whore*, III, i, 179.

162 *barbers' basins.* Metal basins, often hired from barbers, were beaten before carted bawds. See H & S, X, 27.

164 *Thy . . . eggs.* An allusion to the hanging of Mrs Anne Turner on 14 November 1615, for her part in the murder of Sir Thomas Overbury: 'Mistress *Turner*, the first inventress of *yellow Starch*, was executed in a Cobweb Lawn Ruff of that colour at *Tyburn*' (James Howell, *Familiar Letters*, ed. J. Jacobs, 1892, p. 20).

165 *Holborn.* The road from Newgate along which criminals were carted on their way to the gallows at Tyburn.

165–6 *Hounslow Heath.* On which executed felons were often hung in chains.

167 *Colebrook.* A common mis-spelling of Colnbrook, a village west of London. Punning outrageously on 'coal'.

TRIMTRAM
  Mayst thou have a reasonable good spring, for thou art like
  to have many dangerous foul falls!
CHOUGH
  Mayst thou have two ruffs torn in one week!   175
TRIMTRAM
  May spiders only weave thy cobweb-lawn!
CHOUGH
  Mayst thou set up in Rogue Lane!
TRIMTRAM
  Live till thou stink'st in garden-alleys!
CHOUGH
  And die sweetly in Tower-ditch!
PRISS
  I thank you for that, good sir roarer.   180
CHOUGH
  Come, shall we go now, Trim? My father-in-law stays for me
  all this while.
TRIMTRAM
  Nay, I'll serve 'em as we did the tobacco-man: I'll bury 'em
  altogether, and give 'em an epitaph.
CHOUGH
  All together, Trim? why, then the epitaph will be accessary   185
  to the sin.
[TRIMTRAM]
  Alas, he has kept the door all his lifetime; for pity let 'em lie
  together in their graves.
CAPTAIN ALBO
  E'en as thou wilt, Trim, and I thank you too, sir.

174 *falls* (i) autumns (ii) falls from virtue. See II, ii, 166 and note
176 *cobweb-lawn* very fine transparent lawn. See note to l.164
177 *set up* establish a brothel
187–8 *Alas . . . graves* ed. (part of preceding speech in Q1)

---

175 *Mayst . . . week.* A similar reference to 'tearing a poor whore's ruff in a
  bawdy-house' in *2 Henry IV*, II, iv, 139 suggests that the expression
  implied more than mere damage to clothing.
177 *Rogue Lane.* Nickname for Sheer or Shire Lane, which ran south into
  Fleet Street, on account of its reputation for vice (Sugden, p. 434).
178 *garden-alleys.* The many public gardens in London were regular haunts
  of prostitutes, who solicited in their alley ways.
179 *Tower-ditch.* The moat round the Tower of London, usually filled with
  sewage.
187 *kept the door.* Ushered in customers at the brothel door; i.e., been a
  pimp. The expression was common; cf. *Troilus and Cressida*, V, x, 50.

TRIMTRAM

> He that the reason would know, let him hark,   190
> Why these three were buried near Marybone Park;
> These three were a pander, a bawd, and a whore,
> That sucked many dry to the bones before.
> Will you know how they lived? Here't may be read;
> The Low Countries did ever find 'em bread;   195
> They lived by Flushing, by Sluys, and the Groyne,
> Sickened in France, and died under the Line.
> Three letters at last commended 'em hither,
> But the hangman broke one in putting together:
> P was the first, who cries out for a pardon,   200
> O craves his book, yet could not read such a hard one,
> An X was the last, which in conjunction

191 *three* ed. (two Q1)
196 *the Groyne* or Groningen, in Holland; with an obvious pun
197 *in France* i.e., of French disease. See note to l.131
199 *putting together* i.e., putting the letters together to form a word
202 *conjunction* = 'putting together'. A quibble on *conjunction* =
      'copulation' (*OED*, *sb.*, 2.b) may be intended

191 *Marybone Park*. Now Regent's Park, at this time a centre of prosti-
      tution.
193 *sucked . . . bones*. Drained many of their wealth (cf. I, i, 274; IV, i,
      195); glancing at *bone-ache*, 'syphilis' (Partridge, p. 153).
195 *Low Countries*. (i) the Netherlands (ii) the low haunts, the stews (iii) the
      (lower) sexual areas of the body. Cf. *The Comedy of Errors*, III, ii,
      136–7.
196 *Flushing*. Dutch seaport, clearly with a sexual quibble; probably 'at-
      taining orgasm' (cf. *OED*, 'flush', *v.*^{2}, 'to rush out suddenly, to spurt').
      Heywood's use of the pun in *A Challenge for Beauty* (Heywood, V, 16)
      supports this.
196 *Sluys*. Town near Bruges, punning on *sluice* = 'to copulate' (Partridge,
      s.v.).
197 *Line*. Punning dizzily on the following: (i) equator (here appropriate
      because of its unbearable heat and because people were thought to lose
      their hair in fevers caught there) (ii) rope, noose (iii) loin (suggested by
      the pararhyme with 'Groyne') (iv) woman's girdle (cf. *The Tempest*, IV,
      i, 236).
198 *letters*. (i) letters of the alphabet (ii) letters of commendation, the
      equivalent of modern passports.
201 *such . . . one*. Apparently, as Sampson suggests, 'such a hard neck-
      verse': 'a Latin verse printed in black-letter (usually the beginning of
      the 51st psalm) formerly set before one claiming benefit of clergy, by
      reading which he might save his neck' (*OED*).

Was broke by Brandon; and here's the conclusion:
By three trees, three letters; these three, pander, bawd,
    whore,
Now stink below ground, stunk long above before.   205

CHOUGH
So, now we have done with you, remember roaring boys.

TRIMTRAM
Farewell, centaur.

CHOUGH
Farewell, bronstrops.

TRIMTRAM
Farewell, fucus.   *Exeunt* CHOUGH *and* TRIMTRAM

CAPTAIN ALBO
Well, Meg, I will learn to roar, and still maintain the name   210
of captain over these lancepresadoes.

MEG
If thou dost not, mayst thou be buried under the roaring
curse!   *Exeunt*

Act V, Scene i

Enter PHYSICIAN, JANE *as a bride*

PHYSICIAN
Will you be obstinate?

JANE
                    Torment me not,
Thou ling'ring executioner to death,
Greatest disease to nature, that striv'st by art
To make men long a-dying! Your practice is
Upon men's bodies; as men pull roses   5
For their own relish, but to kill the flower,
So you maintain your lives by others' deaths:
What eat you then but carrion?

PHYSICIAN
                    Fie, bitterness;

---

204 *trees* gallowses   211 *lancepresadoes* lancecorporals
  4 *practice* (i) (medical) skill (ii) cunning, deceit
  6 *relish* enjoyment   8 *but* ed. (by Q1)
  8–10 *Fie . . . else* see I, i, 377 and note

---

203 *Brandon.* Gregory Brandon, the common hangman of London.
  2 *ling'ring.* Often used to describe a death painfully protracted; cf. *2*
  Henry VI, III, ii, 247: 'torture him with grievous ling'ring death'.

Y'ad need to candy o'er your tongue a little,
Your words will hardly be digested else.   10

JANE
You can give yourself a vomit to return 'em,
If they offend your stomach.

PHYSICIAN
                              Hear my vow:
You are to be married today—

JANE
                              A second torment,
Worse than the first, 'cause unavoidable.
I would I could as soon annihilate   15
My father's will in that as forbid thy lust!

PHYSICIAN
If you then tender an unwilling hand,
Meet it with revenge—marry a cuckold.

JANE
If thou wilt marry me, I'll make that vow,
And give my body for satisfaction   20
To him that should enjoy me for his wife.

PHYSICIAN
Go to, I'll mar your marriage.

JANE
                              Do, plague me so:
I'll rather bear the brand of all that's past
In capital characters upon my brow,
Than think to be thy whore or marry him.   25

PHYSICIAN
I will defame thee ever.

JANE
                              Spare me not.

PHYSICIAN
I will produce thy bastard,
Bring thee to public penance.

JANE
                              No matter, I care not:

---

11 *vomit* emetic
15 *annihilate* nullify
24 *characters* letters

23–4 *I'll . . . brow.* Whores were sometimes branded on the forehead, and
    this part of the face stood proverbially for the character as signalling
    shame or guilt; cf. *Hamlet*, IV, v, 115 and Tilley, F590.

I shall then have a clean sheet; I'll wear twenty,
Rather than one defiled with thee.
PHYSICIAN

                          Look for revenge!   30
JANE
Pursue it fully then.—[*Aside*] Out of his hate
I shall escape, I hope, a loathed fate.   *Exit* JANE
PHYSICIAN
Am I rejected, all my baits nibbled off,
And not the fish caught? I'll trouble the whole stream,
And choke it in the mud: since hooks not take,   35
I'll throw in nets that shall or kill or break.—
This is the bridegroom's man.—

           Enter TRIMTRAM *with rosemary*

               Hark, sir, a word.

TRIMTRAM
'Tis a busy day, sir, nor I need no physic;
You see I scour about my business.
PHYSICIAN
Pray you a word, sir: your master is to be married today?   40
TRIMTRAM
Else all this rosemary's lost.
PHYSICIAN
I would speak with your master, sir.
TRIMTRAM
My master, sir, is to be married this morning, and cannot be
within while soon at night.

35 *take* catch hold
37 s.d. *rosemary* see IV, i, 200–1 and note
39 *scour* (i) hasten (ii) purge
44 *within . . . night* at home until early this evening (with a bawdy
    double entendre)

———

29 *clean sheet.* Sexual offenders were often made to do public penance
    dressed in white sheets. Punning here on the colloquial sense.
30 *one . . . thee.* As commonly, *sheet* is seen here as symbolizing sexual
    intercourse (see Partridge, *s.v.*). The transition enables Rowley to
    counterpoint in a single image Jane's choice of public humiliation or
    personal defilement.
32 *escape* ed. (pursue Q1). Emendation on the assumption of eye-skip to
    the line above seems the best course. 'Pursue' can, however, make some
    sense if 'loathed fate' is taken as referring to Jane's imminent exposure,
    which she 'hopes' for since it will prevent her marrying Chough.
33–6 *my . . . break.* Taking up Jane's metaphor at III, ii, 122.

PHYSICIAN
    If you will do your master the best service   45
    That e'er you did him; if he shall not curse
    Your negligence hereafter slacking it;
    If he shall bless me for the dearest friend
    That ever his acquaintance met withal;
    Let me speak with him ere he go to church.   50

TRIMTRAM
    A right physician! you would have none go to the church nor
    churchyard till you send them thither: well, if death do not
    spare you yourselves he deals hardly with you, for you are
    better benefactors and send more to him than all diseases
    besides.   55

CHOUGH *within*
    What, Trimtram, Trimtram!

TRIMTRAM
    I come, sir.—Hark you, you may hear him: he's upon the
    spur, and would fain mount the saddle of matrimony; but,
    if I can, I'll persuade him to come to you.

PHYSICIAN
    Pray you do, sir.—   *Exit* TRIMTRAM
                I'll teach all peevish niceness   60
    To beware the strong advantage of revenge.

                Enter CHOUGH

CHOUGH
    Who's that would speak with me?

PHYSICIAN
                     None but a friend, sir;
    I would speak with you.

CHOUGH
    Why, sir, and I dare speak with any man under the universe.
    Can you roar, sir?   65

PHYSICIAN
    No, in faith, sir;
    I come to tell you mildly for your good,
    If you please to hear me. You are upon marriage?

CHOUGH
    No, sir, I am towards it, but not upon it yet.

  60 *peevish niceness* perverse coyness
  69 *am* Q2 (*an* Q1)
     upon it referring to the male's superincumbency in the sexual act

---

  57–8 *he's . . . saddle.* The joke turns on the idea of *riding* = (of a man)
    mounting sexually, copulating.

PHYSICIAN

Do you know what to do?   70

CHOUGH

Yes, sir, I have practised what to do before now; I would be
ashamed to be married else: I have seen a bronstrops in my
time, and a hippocrene, and a tweak too.

PHYSICIAN

Take fair heed, sir; the wife that you would marry
Is not fit for you.   75

CHOUGH

Why, sir, have you tried her?

PHYSICIAN

Not I, believe it, sir; but believe withal
She has been tried.

CHOUGH

Why, sir, is she a fructifer, or a fucus?

PHYSICIAN

All that I speak, sir, is in love to you: 80
Your bride that may be has not that portion
That a bride should have.

CHOUGH

Why, sir, she has a thousand and a better penny.

PHYSICIAN

I do not speak of rubbish, dross, and ore,
But the refined metal, honour, sir.   85

CHOUGH

What she wants in honour shall be made up in worship, sir;
money will purchase both.

PHYSICIAN

To be plain with you, she's nought.   *Draws his sword*

CHOUGH

If thou canst not roar, th'art a dead man! My bride nought?

PHYSICIAN

Sir, I do not fear you that way; what I speak   90
My life shall maintain: I say she's nought.

74–5 *Take . . . you* prose in Q1   81 *portion* dowry
81–2 *Your . . . have* prose in Q1   84 *dross . . . ore* see II, ii, 131
86 *worship* outward honour, esteem
88 *nought* immoral, unchaste

89 Previous editors direct Chough to draw his sword here, but his failure
   to do so is implied by l.94. He shows the same reluctance at IV, i, 158.
90–1 *what . . . maintain.* A standard formula in duelling etiquette; cf
   1 Henry IV, IV, iii, 9, and note the Colonel's retort at I, i, 349.

CHOUGH
   Dost thou not fear me?
PHYSICIAN
   Indeed I do not, sir.
CHOUGH
   I'll never draw upon thee while I live for that trick. Put up
   and speak freely.   95
PHYSICIAN
   Your intended bride is a whore; that's freely, sir.
CHOUGH
   Yes, faith, a whore's free enough, and she hath a conscience.
   Is she a whore? Foot, I warrant she has the pox then!
PHYSICIAN
   Worse, the plague; 'tis more incurable.
CHOUGH
   A plaguy whore? a pox on her, I'll none of her!   100
PHYSICIAN
   Mine accusation shall have firm evidence;
   I will produce an unavoided witness,
   A bastard of her bearing.
CHOUGH
   A bastard? 'snails, there's great suspicion she's a whore
   then! I'll wrestle a fall with her father for putting this trick   105
   upon me, as I am a gentleman.
PHYSICIAN
   Good sir, mistake me not; I do not speak
   To break the contract of united hearts;
   I will not pull that curse upon my head,
   To separate the husband and the wife;   110
   But this, in love, I thought fit to reveal,
   As the due office betwixt man and man,

94 *for that trick* on that account (a colloquial tag)
96 *freely* frankly, plainly
97 *and* if
98 *Foot* oath, short for 'God's foot'
102 *unavoided* irrefutable (*OED*'s only example of this sense)
104 *'snails* God's nails (an oath which Middleton never uses)
112 *office* duty

---

97 *free*. Used 'of a woman that grants a man the freedom of her body'
   (Partridge, *s.v.*).
109–10 *I . . . wife*. Taken from Cooke's comedy *Greene's Tu Quoque*: 'I'll
   not have the crime lie on my head,/To divide man and wife' (W. C.
   Hazlitt, ed., *Dodsley's Old English Plays*, 15 vols., 1874–76, XI, 287).
   Rowley contributed a memorial couplet to the first edition of 1614.

That you might not be ignorant of your ills.
Consider now of my premonishment
As yourself shall please.   115

CHOUGH
I'll burn all the rosemary to sweeten the house, for in my
conscience 'tis infected. Has she drunk bastard? If she
would piss me wine vinegar now nine times a day, I'd never
have her, and I thank you too.

Enter TRIMTRAM

TRIMTRAM
Come, will you come away, sir? They have all rosemary, and   120
stay for you to lead the way.

CHOUGH
I'll not be married today, Trimtram. Hast e'er an almanac
about thee? This is the nineteenth of August: look what day
of the month 'tis.

TRIMTRAM   *Looks in an almanac*
'Tis tenty-nine indeed, sir.   125

CHOUGH
What's the word? what says Bretnor?

TRIMTRAM
The word is, sir, 'There's a hole in her coat'.

CHOUGH
I thought so, the physician agrees with him; I'll not marry
today.

113 *ills* wrongs
114 *premonishment* admonition
116–17 *in my conscience* by my faith, truly (a stock phrase)
125 *tenty-nine* i.e., nineteen
126 *word* motto

---

117 *bastard.* Sweet Spanish wine. The pun is common; cf. *Measure for
    Measure*, III, ii, 4.
122 *almanac.* The credulity of almanac readers was often satirized (cf. *Every
    Man out*, I, iii, 1–64), and with especial frequency by Middleton; e.g.,
    The Puritan, IV, i, 287ff.; the character Weatherwise in *No Wit, No
    Help.*
126 *Bretnor.* Thomas Bretnor, the famous Jacobean almanac-maker, lam-
    pooned as the character Norbrett in Fletcher's *The Bloody Brother.* Cf.
    Middleton's *Inner Temple Masque*, ll.204–6: 'This farmer will not cast
    his seed i' the ground/Before he look in Bretnor; there he finds/Some
    word which he hugs happily, as, *Ply the Box*'.
127 *There's . . . coat.* Her honour is flawed. Proverbial (see Tilley, H522),
    but not used by Bretnor.

TRIMTRAM

    I pray you, sir, there will be charges for new rosemary else;   130
    this will be withered by tomorrow.

CHOUGH

    Make a bonfire on't to sweeten Rosemary Lane. Prithee,
    Trim, entreat my father-in-law that might have been to come
    and speak with me.

TRIMTRAM

    The bride cries already and looks t'other way; and you be so   135
    backward too, we shall have a fine arseward wedding on't.

                             Exit TRIMTRAM

CHOUGH

    You'll stand to your words, sir?

PHYSICIAN

    I'll not fly the house, sir; when you have need, call me to
    evidence.

CHOUGH

    If you'll prove she has borne a bastard, I'll stand to't she's a   140
    whore.   *Exit* PHYSICIAN

            Enter RUSSELL *and* TRIMTRAM

RUSSELL

    Why, how now, son? what causeth these delays?
    All stay for your leading.

CHOUGH

    Came I from the Mount to be confronted?

RUSSELL

    How's that, sir?   145

CHOUGH

    Canst thou roar, old man?

RUSSELL

    Roar? how mean you, sir?

CHOUGH

    Why then, I'll tell thee plainly, thy daughter is a bronstrops.

135 *and* if
136 *backward* reluctant
141 s.d. *Exit* PHYSICIAN ed. (follows l.139 in Q1)
144 *Mount* see II, ii, 135
148 *is* Q2 (in Q1)

132 *Rosemary Lane.* A London street, now Royal Mint Street, of ill repute
    (Sugden).
144 *confronted.* i.e., affronted. Chough's malapropism is prompted by his
    roaring jargon; cf. IV, iv, 55.

RUSSELL

A bronstrop? what's that, sir?

TRIMTRAM

Sir, if she be so, she is a hippocrene.   150

CHOUGH

Nay, worse, she is a fructifer.

TRIMTRAM

Nay then, she is a fucus, a minotaur, and a tweak.

RUSSELL

Pray you speak to my understanding, sir.

CHOUGH

If thou wilt have it in plain terms, she is a calicut and a
panagron.   155

TRIMTRAM

Nay then, she is a duplar and a sindicus.

RUSSELL

Good sir, speak English to me.

CHOUGH

All this is Cornish to thee; I say thy daughter has drunk
bastard in her time.

RUSSELL

Bastard? you do not mean to make her a whore?   160

CHOUGH

Yes, but I do; if she make a fool of me, I'll ne'er make her
my wife till she have her maidenhead again.

RUSSELL

A whore? I do defy this calumny.

CHOUGH

Dost thou? I defy thee then.

TRIMTRAM

Do you, sir?—Then I defy thee too: fight with us both at   165
once in this quarrel, if thou darest!

CHOUGH

I could have had a whore at Plymouth.

TRIMTRAM

Ay, or at Pe'ryn.

CHOUGH

Ay, or under the Mount.

---

149 *bronstrop.* Normalized by other editors; cf. IV, i, 102 and note.

167ff. Places on Chough's itinerary from Cornwall to London.

168 *Pe'ryn.* Penryn, a town in Cornwall near Falmouth.

169 *Mount.* St Michael's Mount, punning on *mons veneris*; cf. *Venus and
Adonis*, l.232.

TRIMTRAM

Or as you came, at Evil.   170

CHOUGH

Or at Hockey Hole in Somersetshire.

TRIMTRAM

Or at the Hanging Stones in Wiltshire.

CHOUGH

Or at Maidenhead in Berkshire. And did I come in by
Maidenhead to go out by Staines?—Oh, that man, woman, or
child would wrestle with me for a pound of patience!   175

RUSSELL

Some thief has put in poison at your ears
To steal the good name of my child from me;
Or if it be a malice of your own,
Be sure I will enforce a proof from you.

CHOUGH

He's a goose and a woodcock that says I will not prove any   180
word that I speak.

TRIMTRAM

Ay, either goose or woodcock; he shall, sir, with any man.

CHOUGH

Phy-si-ci-an! *mauz avez*, physician!

[*Enter* PHYSICIAN]

---

180 *goose . . . woodcock* common terms for a fool

---

170 *came*. Punning on *come* = 'to experience a sexual emission' (Partridge,
s.v.).

170 *Evil*. Yeovil in Somersetshire. The contemporary spelling preserves the
pun.

171 *Hockey Hole*. Wookey Hole, near Wells; for the pun, see II, ii, 209.
Most editors treat Q1's form as an error, but it may be either legitimate
('Ochie-hole' is a comparable instance) or the result of confusion with
Hockley (in the) Hole in London.

172 *Hanging Stones*. Stonehenge, punning on *stones* = 'testicles' (Partridge,
s.v.).

173 *come in*. Playing on the idea of sexual entry.

176 *put . . . ears*. Thought a silent and deadly method of killing; cf. *Hamlet*,
I, v, 63. *Poison* = slander; cf. I, i, 358.

183 *mauz avez*. Chough appears to be saying, in Cornish, 'come along', or
'hurry up'. If so, Rowley probably intends a phonetic approximation of
môs (move, go) and *aves* (out, outside). This is ungrammatical (*môs* in
the imperative is incredibly *kejy* or *kehejy*), but if the way in which
Middleton massacres Welsh in *A Chaste Maid* is anything to go by, one
doubts whether Rowley would have bothered with such distinctions.

RUSSELL
Is he the author?
PHYSICIAN
Sir, with much sorrow for your sorrow's sake,   185
I must deliver this most certain truth:
Your daughter is an honour-stained bride,
Indeed she is the mother to a child
Before the lawful wife unto a husband.
CHOUGH
Law, that's worse than I told thee; I said she had borne a   190
bastard, and he says she was the mother on't too.
RUSSELL
I'm yet an infidel against all this,
And will believe the sun is made of brass,
The stars of amber—
CHOUGH
And the moon of a Holland cheese—   195
RUSSELL
Rather than this impossibility.—Oh, here she comes.

Enter JANE *and* ANNE

Nay, come, daughter, stand at the bar of shame;
Either now quit thyself, or kill me ever;
Your marriage-day is spoiled if all be true.
JANE
A happy misery! who's my accuser?   200
PHYSICIAN
I am, that knows it true I speak.
CHOUGH
Yes, and I'm his witness.
TRIMTRAM
And I.
CHOUGH
And I again.
TRIMTRAM
And I again too. There's four; that's enough, I hope.   205
RUSSELL
How can you witness, sir, that nothing know
But what you have received from his report?

190 *Law* see I, i, 182
192 *infidel* i.e., 'unbeliever'
198 *quit* acquit
205 *And . . . hope* lineation ed. (theres . . . hope Q1 as separate line)

CHOUGH

    Must we not believe our physicians? Pray you, think I know
    as much as every fool does.

TRIMTRAM

    Let me be Trimtram:—I pray you too, sir.   210

JANE

    Sir, if this bad man have laid a blemish
    On my white name, he is a most false one,
    Defaming me for the just denial
    Of his foul lust.—Nay, now you shall be known, sir.

ANNE

    Sir, I'm his sister, and do better know him   215
    Than all of you: give not too much belief
    To his wild words; he's oftentimes mad, sir.

PHYSICIAN

    I thank you, good sister.

ANNE

    [*Aside to* PHYSICIAN] Are you not mad to do this office?
    Fie upon your malice!   220

PHYSICIAN

    I'll presently produce both nurse and child,
    Whose very eyes shall call her mother before it speaks. [*Exit*]

CHOUGH

    Ha, ha, ha, ha! by my troth, I'd spend a shilling on that
    condition to hear that. I think in my conscience I shall
    take the physician in a lie: if the child call her mother   225
    before it can speak, I'll never wrestle while I live again.

TRIMTRAM

    It must be a she child if it do, sir; and those speak the
    soonest of any living creatures, they say.

CHOUGH

    Baw, waw! a dog will bark a month sooner; he's a very puppy
    else.   230

RUSSELL

    [*Aside to* JANE] Come, tell truth 'twixt ourselves; here's none
      but friends;
    One spot a father's love will soon wipe off;

212 *white* unsullied, virtuous
224 *in my conscience* see note to l.116
232 *spot* see II, ii, 76 and note

---

210 *Let . . . Trimtram.* i.e., let me be known by my own name rather than
    be classed as a fool (as which Chough has unwittingly classed himself).

The truth, and thereby try my love abundant:
I'll cover it with all the care I have,
And yet, perhaps, make up a marriage-day. 235

JANE
[*Aside to* RUSSELL] Then it's true, sir, I have a child.

RUSSELL

Hast thou?

Well, wipe thine eyes, I'm a grandfather then;
If all bastards were banished, the city would be thin
In the thickest term-time. Well now, let me alone,
I'll try my wits for thee.—Richard, Francis, Andrew! 240
None of my knaves within?

Enter his SERVANT

SERVANT
Here's one of 'em, sir: the guests come in apace.

RUSSELL
Do they, Dick? Let 'em have wine and sugar; we'll be for 'em
presently.—But hark, Dick. [*Whispers to* SERVANT]

CHOUGH
I long to hear this child speak, i'faith, Trim; I would this 245
foolish physician would come at once.

TRIMTRAM
If it calls her mother, I hope it shall never call you father.

CHOUGH
No; and it do, I'll whip it, i'faith, and give thee leave to whip
me.

RUSSELL 250
Run on thy best legs, Dick.

SERVANT
I'll be here in a twinkling, sir. *Exit* SERVANT

Enter PHYSICIAN, NURSE *with the child*

234 *cover* conceal
236 *a child* Q2 (om. a Q1)
241 *knaves* servants
246 *at* ed. (om. Q1) previous editors follow Q1
248 *and it* if it

233 *thereby* ed. (they Q1). Taking *and* = 'if' is a poor alternative to
emendation. In the copy the word was probably abbreviated to 'th^{by}',
and misread by the compositor.
239 *term-time.* One of the four periods of the year during which the
law-courts were in session, when London was crowded with litigants.
243 *sugar.* The English preferred sweetened wines (Sampson).

PHYSICIAN

Now, gentlemen, believe your eyes if not my tongue:
Do not you call this your child?

CHOUGH

Phew, that's not the point: you promised us the child should
call her mother; if it does this month, I'll ne'er go to the   255
roaring-school again.

RUSSELL

Whose child is this, nurse?

NURSE

Dis gentleman's, so he to me readen. *Points to the* PHYSICIAN

CHOUGH

'Snails, she's the physician's bronstrops, Trim!

TRIMTRAM

His fucus, his very tweak, i'faith!   260

CHOUGH

A glister in his teeth! Let him take her with a purgation to
him!

RUSSELL

'Tis as your sister said, you are stark mad, sir;
This much confirms it. You have defamed
Mine honest daughter; I'll have you punished for't,   265
Besides the civil penance of your sin
And keeping of your bastard.

PHYSICIAN

                    This is fine!
All your wit and wealth must not thus carry it.

RUSSELL

Sir Chough, a word with you. [*Speaks aside to* CHOUGH *and*
                                          TRIMTRAM]

CHOUGH

I'll not have her, i'faith, sir; if Trimtram will have her,   270
and he will, let him.

TRIMTRAM

Who, I, sir? I scorn it. If you'll have her, I'll have her too;
I'll do as you do, and no otherwise.

258 *to me readen* informed me (Md. Dutch *raden*)
271 *and* if

261 *A . . . teeth.* A witty nonce-variant of the common rejoinder 'turd in
    your teeth'; *glister* = enema, suppository.
266 *civil penance.* The physician's threat recoils upon him. See I.28.

RUSSELL

I do not mean't so either; this only, sir,
That whatsoe'er y'ave seen, you would be silent: 275
Hinder not my child of another husband,
Though you forsake her.

CHOUGH

I'll not speak a word, i'faith.

RUSSELL

As you are a gentleman?

CHOUGH

By these basket hilts, as I am a youth,   280
A gentleman, a roarer.

RUSSELL

Charm your man, I beseech you, too.

CHOUGH

I warrant you, sir, he shall do nothing but what I do before
him.

RUSSELL

I shall most dearly thank you.—

Enter SERVANT *with* FITZALLEN

                              Oh, are you come?   285
Welcome, son-in-law! This was beyond your hope:
We old men have pretty conceits sometimes;
Your wedding-day's prepared, and this is it:
How think you of it?

FITZALLEN

                    As of the joyfull'st
That ever welcomed me! You show yourself now   290
A pattern to all kind fathers.—My sweetest Jane!

RUSSELL

Your captivity I meant but as a sauce

282 *Charm* i.e., charm his tongue. Cf. *OED*, *v.*, 4
287 *pretty conceits* ingenious fancies

---

274 *mean't so* ed. (meant to Q1 meane to Q2). Previous editors read 'mean't
   to', which makes no sense. Accepting Q2 would entail re-assigning
   'I . . . either' to Chough.
280 *basket hilts.* Hilt of narrow metal plates curved into the shape of a
   basket. As the hilt was divided into three parts—pommel, handle, and
   shell—it was often spoken of as plural. To swear upon one's sword (a
   kind of cross) was a regular form of oath; cf. l.300.
292 *sauce.* Cf. Rowley's *A Shoemaker*, III, ii, 109: 'If I endure a rough
   chiding for my paines,/It is but sawce to sweete meates'.

Unto your wedding-dinner; now I'm sure
'Tis far more welcome in this short restraint
Than had it freely come.

FITZALLEN

                     A thousandfold.   295

JANE

     [*Aside*] I like this well.

CHOUGH

     [*Aside to* TRIMTRAM] I have not the heart to see this gentle-
man gulled so; I will reveal. I make it mine own case: 'tis a
foul case.

TRIMTRAM

     Remember you have sworn by your hilts.   300

CHOUGH

     I'll break my hilts rather than conceal. I have a trick: do
thou follow me; I will reveal it, and yet not speak it neither.

TRIMTRAM

     'Tis my duty to follow you, sir.

CHOUGH *sings*

     Take heed in time, oh man, unto thy head.

TRIMTRAM *sings*

     All is not gold that glistereth in bed.   305

RUSSELL

     Why, sir! why, sir!

CHOUGH

     Look to't, I say, thy bride's a bronstrops.

TRIMTRAM

     And knows the thing that men wear in their slops.

FITZALLEN

     How's this, sir?

CHOUGH

     A hippocrene, a tweak, for and a fucus.   310

TRIMTRAM

     Let not fond love with foretops so rebuke us.

---

298 *gulled* duped
304 *head* where a cuckold's horn may sprout
305 *All . . . bed* cf. 'All is not gold that glisters' (Tilley, A146)
311 *fond* foolish
     foretops forelocks (meaning cuckolds' horns)

298–9 *case . . . case.* Punning on the sense 'vagina' (see Partridge, *s.v.*).
308 *slops.* Wide baggy trousers, illustrated on the title-page of Q1.
310 *for and.* 'And moreover', a line-filler common in songs; cf. *Hamlet*, V, i,
     92.

RUSSELL
  Good sir!
CHOUGH
  Behold a baby of this maid's begetting.
TRIMTRAM
  A deed of darkness after the sunsetting.
RUSSELL
  Your oath, sir!   315
CHOUGH
  I swear and sing thy bride has taken physic.
TRIMTRAM
  This was the doctor cured her of that phthisic.
CHOUGH
  If you'll believe me, I will say no more.
TRIMTRAM
  Thy bride's a tweak, as we do say that roar.
CHOUGH
  Bear witness, gentlemen, I have not spoke a word: 320
  My hilts are whole still.
FITZALLEN
  This is a sweet epithalamium
  Unto the marriage-bed, a musical,
  Harmonious Io! Sir, y'ave wronged me,
  And basely wronged me: was this your cunning fetch,   325
  To fetch me out of prison, forever
  To marry me unto a strumpet?
RUSSELL
  None of those words, good sir;
  'Tis but a fault, and 'tis a sweet one too.
  Come, sir, your means is short, lengthen your fortunes   330
  With a fair proffer: I'll put a thousand pieces
  Into the scale, to help her to weigh it up,
  Above the first dowry.

---

314 *of darkness* (i) evil (ii) performed in the dark
317 *phthisic* strictly, pulmonary consumption; at this time often used
    loosely for a severe cough
325 *fetch* stratagem

---

324 *Io.* Exclamation of joy or triumph, sometimes used as a noun to mean
    'exultant song' (*OED*). Perhaps conventionally associated with wed-
    dings; cf. Marston, *Antonio's Revenge*, IV, iv, p. 127: '*Io* to *Hymen*'.
330 *short.* Cf. *Timon of Athens*, I, i, 99: 'His means most short, his creditors
    most strait'. Russell characteristically quibbles on the literal sense.

FITZALLEN
                    Ha? you say well,
  Shame may be bought out at a dear rate;
  A thousand pieces added to her dowry!   335
RUSSELL [*Giving money*]
  There's five hundred of 'em to make the bargain.
  I have worthy guests coming, and would not delude 'em;
  Say: speak like a son to me.
FITZALLEN
                  Your blessing, sir,
  We are both yours.—Witness, gentlemen,
  These must be made up a thousand pieces,   340
  Added to a first thousand for her dowry,
  To father that child.
PHYSICIAN
             Oh, is it out now?
CHOUGH
  For t'other thousand I'll do't myself yet.
TRIMTRAM
  Or I, if my master will.
FITZALLEN
  The bargain's made, sir, I have the tender   345
  And possession both, and will keep my purchase.
CHOUGH
  Take her e'en to you with all her moveables; I'll wear my
  bachelors' buttons still.
TRIMTRAM
  So will I, i'faith; they are the best flowers in any man's
  garden, next to heart's-ease.   350
FITZALLEN
  [*Takes up the child*] This is as welcome as the other, sir,
  And both as the best bliss that e'er on earth
  I shall enjoy. Sir, this is mine own child,

336 *make* seal
337 *delude* disappoint
338–42 *Your . . . child* prose in Q1
340 *made up* made up to
345 *tender* formal offer
347 *moveables* personal property (with an obscene innuendo)
350 *heart's-ease* a name for the pansy

---

348 *bachelors' buttons.* A name for the campion. Flower-name puns are
    another of Rowley's trade-marks; cf. *All's Lost by Lust*, III, iii, 107; *A
    New Wonder*, III, i, p. 144.

You could not have found out a fitter father;
Nor is it basely bred, as you imagine,   355
For we were wedded by the hand of heaven
Ere this work was begun.

CHOUGH
At Pancridge, I'll lay my life on't.

TRIMTRAM
I'll lay my life on't too, 'twas there.

FITZALLEN
Somewhere it was, sir.

RUSSELL
                              Was't so, i'faith, son?   360

JANE
And that I must have revealed to you, sir,
Ere I had gone to church with this fair groom;
But thank this gentleman, he prevented me.—
I am much bound unto your malice, sir.

PHYSICIAN
I am ashamed.

JANE
                              Shame to amendment then.   365

RUSSELL
Now get you together for a couple of cunning ones!
But son, a word: the latter thousand pieces
Is now more than bargain.

FITZALLEN
                              No, by my faith, sir,
Here's witness enough on't; 'must serve to pay my fees,
Imprisonment is costly.   370

CHOUGH
By my troth, the old man has gulled himself finely! Well,

---

363 *prevented* anticipated

358 *Pancridge*. Or (St) Pancras, a disreputable suburb south of Cheapside.
    'It seems to have been often used for hasty and irregular marriages'
    (Sugden, p. 387).
361 *And . . . you*. Cf. H. Swinburne, *A Treatise of Spousals*, 1686, p. 13: 'if
    either of [a couple bound by a *de praesenti* contract] should in fact proceed
    to solemnize Matrimony with any other person . . . This Matrimony is
    to be dissolved as unlawful, the Parties marrying to be punished as
    Adulterers, and their Issue in danger of *Bastardy*'.
368 *bargain*. Most editors supply 'the', but the usage is common; cf. *1
    Henry IV*, III, i, 139.
369 *fees*. Prisoners were required to pay their own food and lodging.

sir, I'll bid myself a guest, though not a groom; I'll dine,
and dance, and roar at the wedding for all this.

TRIMTRAM

So will I, sir, if my master does.

RUSSELL

Well, sir, you are welcome; but now no more words on't   375
Till we be set at dinner, for there will mirth
Be the most useful for digestion.
See, my best guests are coming.

Enter CAPTAIN AGER, SURGEON, LADY AGER,
COLONEL'S SISTER, [CAPTAIN AGER's] *two* FRIENDS

CAPTAIN AGER

Recovered, say'st thou?

SURGEON

May I be excluded quite out of Surgeons' Hall else! Marry,   380
I must tell you the wound was fain to be twice corroded;
'twas a plain gastroraphy, and a deep one; but I closed the
lips on't with bandages and sutures, which is a kind conjunction of the parts separated against the course of nature.

CAPTAIN AGER

Well, sir, he is well.   385

SURGEON

I feared him, I assure you, Captain; before the suture in the
belly, it grew almost to a convulsion, and there was like to
be a bloody issue from the hollow vessels of the kidneys.

---

372 *bid* invite
383 *kind* natural

---

380 *Surgeons' Hall.* Barber-Surgeons' Hall in Monkswell Street,
Cripplegate.
381 *was . . . corroded.* Inclined twice to corrosion. The sense in which the
authors found *corroded* in Lowe, 'eaten away', proves Sampson's gloss,
'cauterized', incorrect.
382 *gastroraphy* ed. (Gastrolophe Q1). Properly, a suture for a belly-wound
(as used in Lowe), but here applied to the wound itself. The dramatists
probably misunderstood Lowe, though possibly they were aware that
the term could be thus loosely employed: 'in common acceptation
[gastroraphy] implies that the Wound of the Belly is complicated with
another of the Intestine' (S. Sharp, *A Treatise of the Operations of
Surgery*, 1739, p. 9).
388 *hollow . . . kidneys.* Arteries and veins taking the blood to and from the
kidneys.

CAPTAIN AGER

There's that, to thank thy news and thy art together.

Gives him money

SURGEON

And if your worship at any time stand in need of incision, if   390
it be your fortune to light into my hands, I'll give you the
best.

CAPTAIN AGER

Uncle, the noble Colonel's recovered.

RUSSELL

Recovered?

Then honour is not dead in all parts, coz.

Enter COLONEL *with his two* FRIENDS

1 CAPTAIN'S FRIEND

Behold him yonder, sir.   395

CAPTAIN AGER

My much unworthiness is now found out;
Th'ast not a face to fit it.

1 COLONEL'S FRIEND

Sir, yonder's Captain Ager.

COLONEL

Oh lieutenant, the wrong I have done his fame
Puts me to silence; shame so confounds me   400
That I dare not see him.

CAPTAIN AGER

I never knew how poor my deserts were
Till he appeared. No way to give requital!
Here, shame me lastingly, do't with his own;
Return this to him, tell him I have riches   405
In that abundance in his sister's love
These come but to oppress me, and confound
All my deservings everlastingly;
I never shall requite my wealth in her, say.
          [*Gives will to* 1 FRIEND, *who takes it to the* COLONEL]
How soon from virtue and an honoured spirit   410
May man receive what he may never merit!

COLONEL

This comes most happily to express me better,
For since this will was made there fell to me

___

399 *fame* reputation

The manor of Fitzdale; give 'em that too:

[Returns will with other papers]

He's like to have charge,   415
There's fair hope of my sister's fruitfulness;
For me I never mean to change my mistress,
And war is able to maintain her servant.

1 CAPTAIN'S FRIEND

Read there, a fair increase, sir, by my faith;
He hath sent it back, sir, with new additions.   420

CAPTAIN AGER

How miserable he makes me! This enforces me
To break through all the passages of shame,
And headlong fall—

COLONEL

                    Into my arms, dear worthy!

CAPTAIN AGER

You have a goodness
Has put me past my answers; you may speak   425
What you please now, I must be silent ever.

COLONEL

This day has shown me joy's unvalued treasure;
I would not change this brotherhood with a monarch;
Into which blessed alliance sacred heaven
Has placed my kinsman, and given him his ends: 430
Fair be that quarrel makes such happy friends!

Exeunt OMNES

FINIS

415 *He's . . . charge* he is well suited to be the owner (*OED*, 'like', *a.*,
        6.a)
415–17 *He's . . . mistress* lineation ed.
425 *Has . . . answers* which has left me no longer capable of replying
427 *unvalued* invaluable   430 *my kinsman* Fitzallen

---

414 *'em* ed. (h'um Q1). Previous editors emend silently to 'him', which is
    less appropriate: the Colonel's sister is on stage as well as Ager, and it
    is she who is the nominee of the will. The Q1 reading is readily
    explained as a confusion of *'um* and *'hem*, both current forms of the
    contraction.
417–18 *For . . . servant.* Military service was often spoken of as a mistress;
    cf. III, i, 55 and *More Dissemblers*, II, iii, 97–8: 'I like not him that has
    two mistresses,/War and his sweetheart; he can ne'er please both'.
    Servant puns on the domestic and romantic senses; cf. III, i, 48.
422 *passages.* 'Interchanges', as at I, i, 155, is preferable to 'acts, actions',
    though either sense is possible; cf. 'passage of arms'.

Printed in Great Britain by
The Garden City Press Limited, Letchworth, Hertfordshire, SG6 1JS